RETURN TO HYPERBOREA

η επιστροφή στην
υπερβορεία

RETURN TO HYPERBOREA

The Heroic Initiate

Written by Tom Billinge

Published by Sanctus Arya Press

Paperback: 979-8-9896441-6-2

Hardcover: 979-8-9896441-7-9

Library of Congress Number pending.

Editing and layout by Benjamin Sieghart.

Cover art (*Orpheus and Apollon* and back cover) by Skinless Frank.

Inside illustrations (*Orpheus, Mysteries,* and *Männerbund*) by Ben Ervin.

Inside map taken from the public domain.

More at:

tombillinge.com

sanctusarya.com

Map of ancient Thrace by Abraham Ortelius (London, circa 1608)

Table of Contents

πολλοὶ μὲν ναρθηκοφόροι,
παῦροι δέ τε Βάκχοι

"Many carry the narthex, but
few are Bakkhoi"
Olympiodoros

Acknowledgements

As always, this work would not have been possible without the support of a few key people.

First I would like to thank the scholars who came before me and allowed me access to knowledge that would have been lost to the mists of time. Greats like W. K. C. Guthrie, Walter Otto, and Karl Kerényi have provided me with foundations upon which I can build. In particular, Arthur Versluis has been of particular help, as his work crosses the divide between academia, pure philosophy, and spirituality. His book *Enter the Mysteries* made me decide to go to Samothráki to experience the site for myself.

My editor Benjamin Sieghart is probably the only individual in this world capable of editing my work. His profound understanding and insightful questioning bring out my best. I am grateful for his keen wits and steadfast friendship.

Like *Undying Glory* and *Age of Heroes,* the artwork for this book was created by the talented Skinless Frank (cover) and Ben Ervin (illustrations). I am greatly indebted to them for their renderings of my ideas into visual form.

My mother Anastasia imbued my siblings and I with a deep sense of Greekness, a cultural debt that I will continue to pay for my entire life. My father Mark is a source of deep inspiration and his encouragement from childhood to this day are irreplaceable. He always reads my initial draft and gives me critical feedback. I owe much to him.

My wife Kristin is a remarkable human being. I am free to explore avenues of interest, travel to ancient Mystery sites in the far-flung corners of Greece, and disappear for several weeks on end because of her unwavering support. My Spiritual debt to her is unfathomable.

Note on Spellings

I have used a Greek polytonic transliteration of almost all Greek names and words. I have done this as I hope to inspire my reader to use the original pronunciation. Words are magic spells. In the ancient Mysteries the language was unknown to the initiates, but they used it anyway because of the power contained in the words and formulas. I hope that the "magical spelling" of the words invokes the ancient power of the Greek initiatic experience.

Some examples of this are:

Hades is rendered Hā́idēs
Centaur is rendered kentaur
Thrace is rendered Thraki
Psyche is rendered psykhḗ
Jason is rendered Iásōn

Prelude

This book works on the premise of the Indo-European *Männerbund* in its Greek incarnation. The *Männerbund*, or "Men's Association," is the group of male warriors comprised mostly of young men on the verge of becoming fully-fledged members of their societies. This phenomenon was found throughout the Indo-European diaspora, as the tradition spread from their original homeland into the various areas they settled in.

An argument has been made by numerous scholars that this is the entire basis of the "Indo-European Migration." The premise is that these groups of young men left their father societies to go further afield and expand their territory into new areas where they would come to dominate.

The initial idea of the *Männerbund* was that the young men were required to go through rites of passage that would put them in the wilderness and on the frontiers of their society as militia and raiding parties. The Greeks formalised this in the classical era as the Athenian *ephēboi* and Spartan *kryptai*. This tradition emerged from much older roots, which this work seeks to examine.

The totemic animal of the Indo-European *Männerbund*, regardless the geographic location it dispersed to, was almost uniformly the wolf. While the Germanic *berserker* (*"bear-shirt"*) or *ulfheðinn* (*"wolf-skin"*) tradition is the one with which most are familiar, the work of Swedish Iranologist Stig Wikander – particularly his *Aryan Männerbund* – demonstrates convincingly the Indian and Iranian aspects of this "Wolf Cult" phenomenon.

The wolf has mainly been the totem of the *Männerbund* because it encapsulates their entire mode of existence. They live in organised hierarchies on the edge of human society, working in bands to raid herds. They likewise are swift and "invisible," travelling between the realms of living and dead.

This book looks specifically at the Greek expression of a *Northern Mystery Tradition* rooted in the concept of a sacred primal warband. It aims to provide a framework for men seeking to become a contemporary heroic initiate of this great and ancient Indo-European Wolf Cult. It is an ageless alchemical quest; a winding, yet elevated path ultimately returning the seeker to Hyperborea and the Holy Summit beyond the gods.

Introduction

The journey that lies ahead of the seeker is long and tortuous; it is not for the fainthearted. It requires foreknowledge of the stops along the way and a spiritual map with an accompanying key. Unfortunately for modern man, there is no longer a living initiatory tradition to prepare him for the experience.

What is in our favour is that the guide has never invented anything new. He merely sees what mortal men cannot and points out the previously invisible. The Truth is still accessible from within. As the seventh century BCE Spartan poet Alkman stated, *"To yearn for yourself is the beginning of learning."*

The ancient initiatory tradition that guided elite men for millennia was the Wolf Cult. Religions changed, technology changed, language changed, rulers changed, laws changed, society changed – but the Wolf Cult did not. It adapted and remained true to its mission no matter what happened outside of it.

The Wolf Cult initiated men to tread the Path of the Holy Warrior. At the heart of this tradition is the initiator shaman. It is he who turns boys into wolves, then wolves into men.

The initiator helps these young wolves begin the Return to Hyperborea. This is not a rational journey. It requires the visionary possession of Apollon the Wolf God and the irrational, untranslatable perception of the other.

The mantic and prophetic incubation rewards the seeker with the cosmological and metaphysical second sight of one who has returned to the source and seen the Absolute. The initiator is not an interpreter. He is the evocator of an imagery-rich mythologem through his cosmogonic and theogonic song.

The Wolf Initiate can gain two levels of second sight to aid him in his Return to Hyperborea. Dionysian cosmological sight is the shamanic vision of twilight realms and spirit animals. It is the eye penetrating the invisible veil, revealing what lies in the mist and Underworldly murk of material existence.

Apollonian metaphysical sight is the transcendent clarity of seeing existence entirely, and directly perceiving the Absolute. It allows the seeker to enter a Hyperborean state of complete ascension in the True North. Both cosmological and metaphysical sight are present in a complete archaic religion. One without the other is an incomplete picture of the Truth of reality.

The exoteric dualism – symbolised for example by the Lapithes and kentaurs – pits Apollon's children against those of Dionysos, the Hyperborean against Telluric, the Master of the

Wolf against the Wolf. This apparent dualism of Dionysian and Apollonian visions is dissolved and unified in the shamanic initiator from Thraki: Orpheus – the hero who lives in both shadow and light. This ancient Thrakian figure entered into Greece before the Greeks were Greek. He brought with him the initiation that became the Mystery religions of antiquity, a diluted form of the original Orphic Hyperborean Wolf Initiation.

Orpheus guides the initiate through states of terror and confusion in the darkness; then, Divine Light dawns and he is admitted into the Realm of Light where he sees sacred visions. These cosmological and metaphysical sights open the *Kosmos* to him. He is more than man, more than wolf; he is both and neither at the same time. He is what some would call a werewolf: a wolf-man who, like the wolf, is able to travel between worlds and return with knowledge. He is able to harness the ferocious and cunning power of the wolf when he and his pack of warriors must allow their animal sides to take control; however he is also able to be a functioning member of society. He is never a lone wolf (a savage and dangerous animal), but always a member of the pack – always a man.

In order to access the ancient Hyperborean Wolf Cult initiation, we must examine the corrupted later forms of Orphism along with its associated mythology, as well as the ancient Mysteries of Eleusís and Samothráki. The original tantric nature of these traditions – with multiple deities and the fundamental unity of the divine presence – are akin to the Eastern Hindu and Buddhist tantras.

Both Pythagoreanism and Orphism are later, degenerated religions of the masses. The Aristocratic Apollonian element faded from Pythagoreanism, and Dionysian elements were accentuated in the Orphic. The Mysteries regressed from an elite initiation to allowing almost anyone to participate.

Despite this, the modern seeker can draw from the same eternal well of inspiration. He does so by peering through the murk to the brightness able to shine through to one who walks the Path of Return. The process of *anámnesis* ("remembering") can still be performed despite heavy layers of dark mist obscuring the original golden light in this Age of Iron.

Beyond the darkness is the Light of Hyperborea on the edge of the material *Kosmos*. Glimmers of the golden immortal realm glisten through fragments of arcane wisdom that survive in the works of ancient writers. Pindar gives a description of Hyperborea in his ode *Pythian 10*:

"...Of the fairest glories that mortals may attain, to him is given to sail to the furthest bound. Yet neither ship nor marching feet may find the wondrous way to the gatherings of the Hyperborean people. Yet was it with these that Perseus the warrior chief once feasted, entering their homes, and chanced upon their sacrifices unto the god, those famous offerings of hecatombs of asses; for in their banquets and rich praise Apollon greatly delights, and laughs to see the rampant lewdness of those brutish beasts. Nor is the Muse a stranger to their life, but on all sides the feet of maidens dancing, the full tones of the lyre and

pealing flutes are all astir; with leaves of gleaming laurel bound upon their hair, they throng with happy hearts to join the revel. Illness and wasting old age visit not this hallowed race, but far from toil and battle they dwell secure from fate's remorseless vengeance..."

The psychonaut Aristéas of Prokonnesos went on a shamanic spirit journey, bringing back with him much about the Hyperboreans and their neighbours. His lost poem the *Arimaspeia* contained descriptions of his Spirit journey to the True North, which ancient writers such as Hēródotos drew from. It is perhaps from the *Arimaspeia* that Pherénikos gets his information.

"And about the Hyperboreans, who inhabit the edge of the world close by the temple of Apollon, and know not war. They, poets sing, sprung from the blood of the Titans of old settled beyond the limpid course of Boreas." (Pherénikos fragment preserved in the Scholia of Pindar *Olympian 1*, 3.23)

Aristéas' journey was later than that of Orpheus, who brought the Hyperborean initiatic mysteries with him from Thraki to the north of Greece. These rites travelled south from the Hyperboreans, who always sent an offering of first fruits to Apollon on Delos for the *Thargelia* festival at the beginning of June. The offering travelled along the migration route the Greeks' Indo-European ancestors took to enter their new land. It passed from the Hyperboreans, to the one-eyed Arimaspians who stole the gryphons' gold, to the Issedonians, to the Skythians, then through various tribes until reaching the Greeks.

An account of this is found in Hēródotos' *Histories* 4.33:

"…*Concerning the Hyperborean people, neither the Skythians nor any other inhabitants of these lands tell us anything, except perhaps the Issedones. And, I think, even they say nothing; for if they did, then the Skythians, too, would have told, just as they tell of the one-eyed men. But Hesiod speaks of Hyperboreans, and Homer too in his poem The Epigonoi, if that is truly the work of Homer. But the Delians say much more about them than any others do. They say that offerings wrapped in straw are brought from the Hyperboreans to Skythia; when these have passed Skythia, each nation in turn receives them from its neighbours until they are carried to the Adriatic Sea, which is the most westerly limit of their journey; from there, they are brought on to the south, the people of Dodona being the first Greeks to receive them. From Dodona they come down to the Melian gulf, and are carried across to Euboia, and one city sends them on to another until they come to Karystos; after this, Andros is left out of their journey, for Karystians carry them to Tenos, and Tenians to Delos. Thus they say these offerings come to Delos.*

"*But on the first journey, the Hyperboreans sent two maidens bearing the offerings, to whom the Delians give the names Hyperokhe and Laodike, and five men of their people with them as escort for safe conduct, those who are now called Perpherees and greatly honoured at Delos. But when those whom they sent never returned, they took it amiss that they should be condemned always to be sending people and not getting them back, and so they carry the offerings, wrapped in straw, to their borders, and tell their neighbours to send them on from*

19

their own country to the next; and the offerings, it is said, come by this conveyance to Delos. I can say of my own knowledge that there is a custom like these offerings; namely, that when the Thrakian and Paionian women sacrifice to the Royal Artemis, they have straw with them while they sacrifice."

The Thakians are said to have come to Thraki from Phrygia in Asia Minor in the 2nd millennium BCE. These Indo-European Steppe raiders share much in common with the Dorians who invaded Greece and pushed their Akhaian cousins across to the east. The Thrakians were well-known for their "barbaric" way of life, choosing to live in small semi-mobile communities rather than establish cities. Their horsemanship was exceptional and even the great hero of the Iliad, Akhilleus, has ties to them as he came from a nameless northern place that Homer conveniently called Phthia. In *Age of Heroes* the Akhaians of the Trojan War are identified as Steppe raiders, Wolf Warriors of deep antiquity. The Thrakians of Orpheus were of the same stock, and it is through their prophet the Wolf Cult initiation survived for a while in Greece before its corruption into a popular cult for the disenfranchised masses.

These Thrakians used Homeric burial practices and worshipped ancient gods in rock sanctuaries significantly older than Mesopotamian and Egyptian temples. They worshipped several gods including the Mountain Mother of the Phrygians, as well as Sabazios and Zalmoxis. Zalmoxis, whose name derives from the Thrakian word *zalmos*, meaning "bearskin" was linked specifically to warriors.

Hēródotos says the Gétai tribe worshipped Zalmoxis and had a belief that "made men immortal." They believed Zalmoxis lived in a cavernous mountain, and that all the dead of their race would one day gather there for immortal life. They said they would return from the other world to this and that their immortal "soul" would be reincarnated.

Ancient writers say Zalmoxis was also the name of the slave and pupil of Pythagóras, while some observers say Pythagóras was a pupil of Zalmoxis. This is a fabrication that connects the Thrakian soul belief and Pythagoreanism. It reinforces the lineage of the ancient wisdom and where it comes from. Reincarnation was a strong Thrakian belief. Thrakians faced death in battle joyfully, knowing the soul could then be freed to a higher existence.

Ekstasis brought the Thrakians an understanding of a second, eternal, divine Self independent of the body. This direct experience of the divine – beyond what intellectualism can perceive or understand – came to them through their other main god Sabazios. Hēródotos says Dionysos is Thrakian; he is thinking of Sabazios, who is a northern reflex of the same god. The Original Dionysos is "Lord of Spirits and Souls of the Dead" who infects worshippers with divine mania. The later wine god is a degeneration: drunkeness is different from "madness."

The initiation festivals of the Thrakian deities involved dance to purge emotional states. Through the rituals, *ekstasis* was elevated to a higher purpose and used in service to the gods. Raging over the mountains in a bakkhic frenzy, purgation of the ecstatically-charged Spirit was a defining characteristic of Dionysos worship in Greece. Dionysos as Bakkheos awoke holy madness; he and Thrakian god Sabazios were one and the same. This god was known to Greeks before arriving in what would become their homeland, as they came from the same origins as the Thrakians and passed through Thraki while journeying.

The Phrygian worship of the Mountain Wolf Mother Kybele was performed on mountain tops in the darkness with torches. Drums and the *aulos* (double flute) accompanied frenzied dance. Worshippers wore fox and doe skins with their hair loose, carrying snakes sacred to Sabazios. They wore horns to emulate the "bull god" and through mania entered into union with the god, becoming Sabazios.

The setting, and in particular the *aulos,* made the worshippers *entheoi* ("full of the god"). Thus the person was "possessed;" he was "abroad" having left his body in a state of *ekstasis.* This was *hieromania,* a sacred madness in which the Spirit winged its way to the god in a state of *enthousiasmos.*

Associated with both Apollon and Dionysos, Thrakian poet-seer Orpheus carried with him the weight of an ancient and profound Northern tradition. He initiated the elite into the Hyperborean Wolf Cult. This initiation is still alive, surviving through the fragments left to us by the ancients. There remains a clear path of ascent for those wishing to Return to Hyperborea.

Part I: Orpheus

Ὀρφεύς

Orpheus

The mysterious figure of "Famous Orpheus" has come down to us as a somewhat effeminate musician who plays his music for the creatures of the forest. He does not fit into the classic Western hero archetype, since he displays no martial characteristics. Instead, he is a priestly figure connected to both Apollon and Dionysos.

While he embodies Apollonian characteristics, he is later associated with Dionysian mystery religions. This is not his original role, which changed as the Thrakian became tamed over centuries into the figure we associate with Orpheus today. The impact of the magical singer related with charms, spells, and incantations was so powerful that his name was used to conjure for over a thousand years throughout classical antiquity.

To search for Orpheus is to chase shadows and grasp at phantoms. He was considered so ancient in antiquity that he was sometimes regarded as the inventor of writing – sometimes so ancient he couldn't have used writing. Plutarch mentions a *xoanon* of Orpheus in Makedonia made of Cypress wood. *Xoana* are ancient wooden representations of the gods, older survivals from an archaic period. There are many strands to the Orpheus story, but no single thread. The narrative, like all mythological material, has several iterations; but while fragmented, it can be reassembled into a general myth from the works of later writers such as Strabo, Pausanias, Konon, Valerius Flaccus, Diódōros, and a 4th Century CE anonymous poem entitled *Orpheus*.

The Greeks considered him to be before Homer, but still in the Heroic Age. Sometimes, as the "father of lays" (songs), they made him an ancestor to Homer. As indicated by his Phrygian cap, Orpheus is a Thrakian. He was born to Kalliope ("beautiful-voiced"), Muse of epic poetry whose voice creates ecstatic harmony. His father is Oiagros, a Thrakian river god, but sometimes Apollon is his sire.

The lyre is first fashioned by Hermês who gives it to Apollon, who in turn passes it on to Orpheus. Apollon teaches the singer to play the seven-stringed lyre, but Orpheus adds two more strings to honour the nine muses. He achieves great powers through his music and verse, and can enter into communion with the gods. He is able to purify sin and cure diseases, averting the goddess of vengeance Nemesis. Orpheus charms animals and enchants men with his songs. A priest of both Apollon and Dionysos, the poet-magus marries the nymph Eurydikē, whose name "wide-ruling" is an epithet of Persephónē (Queen of the Underworld). Eurydikē is perhaps a later addition, with his original wife a Thrakian nymph called Agriope ("wild-eyed" or "wild-voiced"). Agriope is a Dryad: a wood nymph of the forest.

His wife is killed by a snake bite and transferred to the Underworld. Orpheus wanders until he gets to the Underworld gate at Tairanon. Playing his lyre, he subdues Kerberos and descends into Hāidēs where he charms Persephónē with his song. The infernal queen allows him to revive his wife on condition that he does not look at her until they have returned to the land of the living. As they ascend, Orpheus looks back at the nymph and she is instantly returned to the land of the dead. Thus Orpheus fails to emulate Dionysos raising his mother Semelē.

Orpheus joins Iásōn (Jason) and the rest of the Argonauts on their journey to Kolkhís to retrieve the Golden Fleece. His role in this endeavour is important in the *Argonautika* of Apollionios Rhodios, but enhanced further in the anonymous *Orphic Argonautika* of late antiquity. After returning, he continues to sing to men and beasts in the forests of Thraki. His luring away of men and refusal to initiate women into his rites incites the ire of the Thrakian women.

Orpheus climbs Mount Pangaion ("All-Earth"), between Makedonia and Thraki, to greet the dawn and perform rites for Apollon. Incited by Dionysos, the Bassarides (Mainades), frenzied worshippers of the ecstatic god, tear him apart as they would a sacrificial animal. They then cast his remains into the Hebros River, from whence they float out to sea. Orpheus' head and lyre cast up on the shore of the island of Lesbos. The fisherman who catches them in his net finds the head singing prophecies.

A plague afflicts Thraki and an oracle tells the Thrakians they must find the head of Orpheus and bury it. The lyre is dedicated at the temple of Apollon, who silences the prophesying head stating "cease from the things which are mine!" In one tradition the head is buried and a temple of Bakkhos is raised above it. In another, the head is brought back to Thraki or to the Greek sanctuary at Dion where a great mound is raised. This then becomes the first Hero shrine. At the site, Orpheus is honoured with all the sacrifices and rites accorded to a god and no women may enter.

This mythic narrative evolved over time into the stories that were told in late antiquity. There is much that can be taken from it that give insight into the original nature of Orpheus. At times Orpheus is identical to Apollon, at others he is the Thrakian Dionysos, but he is always separate from them and almost an abstraction of their joint qualities. A gentle hero, free from warlike attributes, Orpheus differs from Apollon in this regard, as the god is also a destructive archer. Calm and peaceful, he differs from Dionysos, who induces madness and violent mania.

Orpheus is a *Theológos*, a singer of divine songs of the gods and *Kosmos*. He is a musician with magical notes who charms nature with his singing. Music and magic were closely associated in the Greek mind. Hermês invented the lyre and is also a magician god. As a psychopomp Orpheus also emulates

27

Hermês by guiding the soul of his beloved from the Underworld. Thus, Orpheus is associated with three gods, but mostly Apollon.

In his Metamorphoses, Ovid says, *"Apollo is the revealer of past, present, and future. He is the bringer of harmony through his lyre."* This is also the strongest characteristic of Orpheus. Apollon's music, like that of Orpheus, also drew wild animals around him. Like Apollon, he is connected to animal husbandry, as he tames wild beasts and embodies the pastoralist. Pindar says that Orpheus was "sent by Apollon" to this world – he is the "Companion of Apollon."

While he induces states of ecstasy, they are not crazed Dionysian states prompted by wine or perhaps Soma. He is an Apollonian ecstatic. Only later does this ecstasy become fully Dionysian in the corrupted Orphic religion. The Greeks believed that in pre-Homeric times he proclaimed to the Thrakians the immortality and divinity of the human soul as well as ritual and moral purity.

The ecstatic side is Apollonian, but his death and his infernal wanderings he owes to Dionysos. Orpheus is somewhat associated with Underworld deities. Like Dionysos, he can intercede with Pluto and Persephónē-Kórē. His wife carries the name Eurydikē, like the epithet of Persephónē, the first mother of Dionysos. Orpheus therefore marries the infernal queen; this is not dissimilar to Odysseus living with Kirke and Kalypso in the *Odyssey*. Both Orpheus and Odysseus are Northern figures.

A mortal marrying the Queen of the Dead or an underworld figure is common also in Celtic folklore. In his death, Orpheus is torn asunder like in the omophagia, the violent Dionysian communion. Despite being torn apart, Orpheus (like Dionysos-Zagreus) lives on.

His head continues to give oracles, much like the head of Mímir in Germanic myth. In the Odinic tradition, the head of a dead soothsayer can speak and tell the future. This is a crumb of a Northern shamanic connection. Orpheus came down into Thraki from the North, from the Original Greek homeland with the Indo-European people. He was an initiator priest of Hyperborean Apollon, of Apollon Lykeios. Orpheus is Hyperborean: a shaman from the distant North who can cross between worlds and sing the magical song of the *Kosmos*.

According to Varro, the Pythagorean poet Ennius spoke of the *kratēr* (cauldron) of Apollon between earth and heaven. This *kratēr* is the centre and boundary between heaven and earth, immortality and birth, life and death, good and evil. Plutarch assigns the *kratēr* as the supernatural tripod of Apollon, connected to the Delphic tripod through Mount Parnassos that intersects the cosmic *kratēr*. It is expressly stated that dreams and images come from *kratēr*. The return of Orpheus from Hãidēs also takes place through the same *kratēr*: the tripod of Apollon.

This Orpheus is the Hyperborean shamanic initiator of men into the Apollonian Wolf Cult of the North.

Πυθαγόρας

Pythagóras

Before being able to understand the Orphic religion that clung to the name Orpheus, one must first look briefly at Pythagoreanism (an occidental Brahminism of sorts) and its eponymous founder Pythagóras of Samos. The figures and myths of Pythagóras and Orpheus intersect at various places, and later Orphic and Pythagorean spiritual traditions align so closely that they clearly developed together in the Greek colonies of Kroton and Metapontum.

Ionian philosopher Pythagóras was born on the island of Samos around 570 BCE. In about 530 BCE he settled in the Akhaian colony of Kroton in Southern Italy. He founded an initiatic philosophical school in which members resided communally, kept the inner teachings secret, and lived an ascetic vegetarian lifestyle.

Many Pythagoreans were also Orphics, and both "cults" prospered and developed in the Southern Italian colonies. Kroton was the home of the Orphic religion, and several

Pythagoreans had the name "Orpheus." Ion of Khios says in the 5th century BCE that Pythagóras wrote some pieces under the name of Orpheus.

The god of Pythagóras is Apollon and the Pythagorean "religion" is Apollonian. Pythagóras was known as Son of Apollon or Apollon incarnate, and was sometimes called "Hyperborean Apollon." Even his name is derived from Pytho (a name of Apollon) and *agorá* ("marketplace"), making him Pytho of the public square. This is reflected in the vegetarianism he espoused in order for his followers to emulate the Hyperboreans themselves.

Pythagóras' hagiographical mythos states he had a golden thigh, and like Orpheus descended into Hā́idēs. In a very ancient tradition, Pythagóras remembered all his previous lives, much like the Buddha after his enlightenment. Pythagóras also had an Apollonian revelation: he channelled the god's spiritual force, which flowed through him and his teachings.

Following the death of Pythagóras in around 495 BCE, Pythagoreans split into *Mathēmatikoi* (intellectuals) and *Akusmatikoi* (mystics), each following separate paths of the Pythagorean teachings. Pythagoreanism is expressed in numerical ratios rather than mythology. Orphism is the mystical counterpart to Pythagoreanism in many regards.

In Pythagoreanism, the tetraktys (a triangular figure consisting of ten points arranged in four rows) expresses the generation of numbers from the primal monad, or world egg, symbolizing unity of the Absolute. This generates the dyad, which expresses power, the limit, and the unlimited. The triad is generated next and represents harmony. Finally, the tetrad represents the *Kosmos*.

Both Orphism and Pythagoreanism have a moral dualism. In the latter, the world is a mixture of form, limit, and light, which are good, and formlessness, darkness, and unlimitedness, which are evil.

Experiments in music lead Pythagóras to his understandings of cosmic ratios. He discovered the universe is both *Kosmos* ("order") and *Harmonía* ("being in tune"). He propounded the theory of the "music of the spheres," where humans must bring their being into *Harmonía* with the *Kosmos*.

Disobedience to harmonic laws leads to ugliness: a denial of the divine beauty of cosmic order. *Kosmos* means "ornament" as well as "order." Therefore, the world is adorned with a beautiful natural order. This musical element strongly yokes Pythagóras to both Apollon and Orpheus.

The Pythagorean "soul" is an immortal *daímonaic* being. Each incarnation is governed by past behaviours, much like in the Indic concept of Karma. The goal is to lift the soul from earthly existence and restore it to a free divine state of being: to return it to its supra-mundane origin.

Empedokles, the conscious successor of Pythagóras in the 5th century BCE, proclaimed a transmigration of *daímones*. This is a transmigration of gods, not souls as in the later sense. He talks of the fate of the *daímon* – the Spirit, not the soul.

Empedokles' doctrine is that there are normal humans and then "fallen" divine beings – *daímones* – who are incarnated through human, animal, and plant forms. When the *daímon* is incarnated, it is always as the highest level of human, animal, or plant forms. The noble body is therefore the living shell, or vehicle of a god.

There is no equality of souls, but an aristocratic cycle of generation leading back to the divine state only for the few. He never talks of the many or of all – just those who are kings, noble athletes, and wise men in this life; but in the next are allowed to reach the ancient Islands of the Blessed, the place of heroes related to the gods. This aristocratically emphasised separation of the bearers of spiritual power is necessarily supplemented by an equally underscored, uniform conception of the rest. This has a counterpart in Confucianism where only the noble has a soul.

Pythagóras also embraced the feminine Dēmétēr religion as a counterfoil to the Apollonian. Dēmétēr, the great soul-bearer of Pythagoreans was in their doctrine same as the ancient earth mother Rhea-Kybele. Pythagóras taught of the four female ages as the four goddesses: the virgin is called Kórē, the young woman is called Nýmphē, the mother is called Métēr, and the grandmother is called Maîa. This is propounded much like the

Tantric conception of the goddess in her manifold avatars.

The Pythagoreans were devoted to the cult of the "soul." This cult of the dead was an eminently feminine concern among the Greeks, but it is impossible to separate it from the cult of life in the Pythagorean current. Women were admitted into the ranks of Pythagorean initiates, as they are at the heart of the ongoing eternal rebirth of the Spirit. It is women who gift with a living soul the gods among humans.

This places the aristocratic woman in a unique place, as it is only she who can give birth to a divine being. The Spartan concept of their women being held in higher esteem than the other women in Greek society is on a similar basis. Gorgo, the wife of Leonidas, reportedly stated that they were "the only women that give birth to real men."

These concepts and general understanding of them are important in comprehending the development of the Orphic religion. This was called the *Orphika* in antiquity, but is known by most as Orphism.

Ὀρφικά

Orphism

The "Orphism" that has come down to us was an over-righteous religion that bore the name of Orpheus, but little resemblance to the original Orphic tradition. It was a later corruption of an original pre-Orphic current. The name Orpheus was taken to lend antiquity and credence to a new religion at that time.

The Orphic religion developed from Pythagoreanism and the writings of Onomakritos. He committed the Orphic poems to writing in Athens around the same time as the Homeridai committed Homer's work to paper in the 7th and 6th centuries BCE. Orpheus is like Homer in that regard: he is *daímon* of the poems, hence they are called "poems of Orpheus" or "*Orphiká.*"

This Orphic religion was more of a literary tradition than a religion as we would see it today. It was not a focused faith with a set of clear dogmatic principles. It did contain concepts and morality which were gleaned from its writings by Plato, who employed philosophy, religion, and poetry in his dialogues.

For example, Plato states in his *7th Letter*, "We must ever maintain a real belief in the ancient and sacred stories, which reveal that our soul is immortal, and has judges, and pays the utmost penalties whenever a man is rid of the body."

This is an Orphic concept.

The 6th century BCE was according to later authors the main period of this Orphic activity. However, the sacred literature of 5th and 6th centuries was already considered at the time to be "of great antiquity."

The Greeks believed that in the mountains of Thraki were tablets with the writing of Orpheus. This is mentioned in the *Álkēstis* of Euripides, and the Scholiast on the *Álkēstis* notes the natural philosopher Herakleides stated that they actually existed on Mount Haimos. Euripides was not the only playwright to be influenced by Orphism, and Aristophanes uses the Orphic theogony and concepts in at least three of his plays: *The Birds*, *The Clouds*, and *The Frogs*.

Originally there was no Orphic religion or scripture, but an Orphic initiatory current from which came these *hieroì lógoi* ("sacred stories"). That the details of the *palaioì lógoi* ("ancient stories") don't exactly match, but follow a similar narrative are evidence that it was an initiatic tradition rather than a concrete religion.

The Orphic "religion" developed in Athens and South Italy in the 6th century BCE, particularly in the colonies of Kroton and Metapontum. It absorbed much from Pythagoreanism (an aristocratic Apollonian religion), possibly being promulgated by students of Pythagóras who wanted to use the name Orpheus to lend an air of antiquity to the new religion. Orpheus was already closely associated with the cult of Apollon, and a calm counterfoil to wild Dionysism.

At that time Orpheus was adopted as founder of various mystical sects in the Italian Greek colonies. These southern cults were chthonian in nature, worshipping telluric gods. The Underworld journey is the only aspect connecting the Northern Orpheus to these cults, but his name became attached to them, leading to the later cultic development of Orphism.

The Hellenistic and Roman Orphism lost much of its original character and became a devotional religion. The Orphic current degenerated into the Orphic religion, which was salvationary, promising a paradise of drunken feasting. It was a religion of magic and spells that attracted charlatans. These sold deliverance through rites and incantations, and wrongdoers were allowed to buy redemption.

The original Orphic current was male and women were excluded, as told in the Orpheus mythos. Later "Orphism" allowed women to participate. It was in practice a Dionysiac religion with the likeness of Orpheus attached to it.

The famous *Orphic Hymns* are not even from this "Orphism," but belonged to a late Roman Dionysian mystery cult. Only the hymns to Nyx, Prōtogonos, the Titans, and Eros are Orphic in nature. Orpheus was clearly used as the name of a patron by a degenerate mystery cult of the Christian era, which was heavily influenced by Christianity. This Dionysiac society with Orpheus as its saint probably hailed from Asia Minor, possibly Pergamon.

It has been theorised by the likes of the great classical scholar W. K. C. Guthrie, that worshippers of Dionysos adopted Orpheus to temper the ecstatic energy of their religion. He believed that Orphism was a reform of Dionysiac energy in the direction of Apollonian sanity. This may hold water for the late Roman religion, but does not make sense for the initial Greek development of Orphism.

The original Orphic initiatory tradition did bridge the gap between Dionysian and Apollonian, but one that only existed due to a schism from the original Hyperborean unity of these two gods. Apollon and Dionysos were only considered as opposites in later exoteric belief. The esoteric understanding of the initiate connects these two deities as two strands of the same thread.

Dionysos was god of the Orphic religion and Orpheus was considered its "founder." Other gods were worshipped, but Dionysos was central. The Orphic religion was bakkhic, but Orpheus is not a bakkhic figure.

The only similarity between Orpheus and Dionysos is that they were both torn asunder; Orpheus is Apollonian in almost all other aspects. Like Apollon, Orpheus' music drew wild animals around him. He is calm and orderly. He is called the "Companion of Apollon" and Pindar says Orpheus was "sent by Apollon."

In the ancient world Apollon and Dionysos were not at loggerheads with each other. They shared Delphoi and were closely allied. Dionysos is called *polyonymos* ("many-named") and a late writer addresses Apollon: "at Delphoi they honour thee with double title, calling thee Apollon and Dionysos."

The Orphics identified both Dionysos and Apollon with Helios. This "Helios-Apollon-Dionysos" was their supreme god. Thus, the Orphic tradition is earlier than the polarisation of Apollon and Dionysos. It recognises the connection of the two Northern deities.

Apollon is "god of the Greeks," along with Zeus. In around 2000 BCE, they brought him from the North, invading the peninsula. The Dionysian cult may not have originated in Thraki, but that is from where it took hold and spread into Greece. Dionysos thus also came into Greece from the North.

Apollon and Dionysos allied from an early date. In the *Odyssey*, Odysseus gets the Ismarian wine from Maros – a Thrakian priest of Apollon. Maros lives in the grove of Apollon, but is son of Euanthes, the son of Dionysos. This indicates Apollon and Dionysos were worshipped together in Thraki, which makes sense of the connection of both gods to Thrakian Orpheus.

Apollon and Dionysos are separated aspects of the unified pole, but these polar "opposites" mutually attract in Orphism. It is the same as the concept of magnetism in the Samothrákian Mysteries. This will be explored in a later chapter.

The late Orphism degenerated several ideas from the original Orphic Wolf Cult, but at its heart initiation and purity remained the two key concepts. Since these two ideas remained, by looking at what the late "Orphics" believed, we can perhaps gain insight into the original nature of the Orphic current.

Vegetarianism was a key part of Orphism. The actual prohibitions were on "meat" and wool. They were not permitted to perform animal sacrifice, nor eat "flesh." This can be looked at from many angles.

The view that eating animals was the same as eating one's relatives is possibly a Pythagorean addition based on reincarnation. The prohibition on eating meat has also been seen as the prohibition of the *Omophagia*, a divergence from the pure Dionysiac ritual. The *Omophagia* is the ancient Kretan rite of rending a live bull and eating its raw flesh as a form of the worship of Dionysos.

This element continued in other Dionysian cults. It was practiced by the Mainades in particular. The union of the worshipper with their god by consuming his flesh was adopted from the cult of Dionysos by early Christians as well.

Another way to look at this "vegetarianism" is through the lens of the Wolf Cult. These young men were taken out of society into the forest to fast and be initiated. This placed them outside civilization, unable to participate in it until they had completed their induction.

Unlike Pythagoreans, Orphic vegetarianism referred only to sacrificial animals: cows, sheep, goats, pigs. The sacrifice is a communal function and all these animals are sacrificed before being eaten. Chicken, fish, and game were not prohibited. Young Wolf Warrior initiates in the forest lived on game, not the meat of society.

Wool fillets were also worn during the communal sacrifice. This would explain the prohibition of woolen garments by the Orphics, who shunned society at large.

Orphics believed that union with the god did not happen by consuming his flesh and blood, but was achieved through the purity of life and inner work. This is an original concept from the ancient Orphic current. They did not believe in original "sin," but an innate "impurity." The concern with cleansing and ritual purification is an Indo-European concept found in the Indian Vedas and Iranian Avesta, as well as Roman ritual.

Orphism was not a "moral" or "community" religion, but an individualistic transmigration of the soul: a personal ecstatic practice designed to purify the soul. Rewards and punishments awaited the Orphic after death depending on whether or not he had cultivated his divine element. Orphism's ethic is dependent on its metaphysic – on man's place in the cosmic order. This is possibly original to the earliest initiatic strata.

The central doctrine of Orphism can be summed up in the words of Orpheus' pupil Musaios in the proem of Diogenes Laertios' *Lives and Opinions of Eminent Philosophers*: "Everything comes to be out of One and is resolved into One."

The god Phanes (and later Zeus) contained the seeds of all being within his body. The manifold world emerged from this mixture. Everything once existed all together in Khaos and that Creation was a process of separation and division. At the end of our era, all will return and become reunited in the One.

This is all related in the Orphic Theogony.

η Ὀρφικὴ θεογονία

Orphic Theogony

While Orphism is a late and corrupted amalgam of various European and Asian mystery rites, at its heart is a set of far older myths. These *theogonies* are poems about the creation of the *Kosmos* and gods. Composed by *theologoi* ("singers of the gods"), they contain material that diverges from the classic Hesiodic *Theogony*.

Hesiod's is the only complete surviving theogony, but in antiquity others existed, including those of Akusilaos of Argos, Epimenídes of Krete, and Pherkydes of Syros. The theogony of Orpheus was said to be older than Hesiod's, but we know of it only through later writers and fragments they quoted.

There were three main Orphic creation accounts in antiquity, plus two possible others. The standard version was the *Rhapsodic Theogony*, with other versions by Eudemos, a student of Aristotle, and a version by Heironymos and Hellanikos. A fourth is alluded to in Apollónios Rhódios' Argonautika, and a fifth is mentioned by Alexander of Aphrodisias. All differ, but the central theme is that everything comes from a primal Unity and returns to its source, undergoing separation and division only between the beginning and end. The main narratives are of Eros/Phanes as the principle of life, the creator and creation, Zeus and his son, and Dionysos and the Titans.

The *Rhapsodic Theogony* attempts to consolidate the earliest strata of Orphic thought and is discussed by Presocratic philosophers Empedokles and Heraklitos, who were influenced by Orphic ideas. Neoplatonists made much of the theme of a primitive world order created by Phanes in Time, which was then swallowed by Zeus who created the second world order from himself. They interpreted Phanes' *Kosmos* as the intelligible world of Platonic ideas, while Zeus' age (our time) as that of matter and senses. The Orphics saw Phanes' *Kosmos* as material but older.

The theogonies are ancient in content if not in composition, being recorded in the 6th century BCE, just like the Epics. In the 7th century BCE, the Athenian Epimenídes began writing down these theogonies and poems. The tradition was conservative, so little was changed over time in their oral transmission. The theogonies are initiatic myths; they did not present clear concepts in Orphism, and even less so in their original Orphic form. They depicted images with an inherent ambiguity, neither constructed nor resolved by philosophical thinking. This transforms the experience of nature into a mythologem, leading to the emergence of a new world.

The initiator, the *theológos* Orpheus, was certainly not an interpreter. He was the evocator of an imagery-rich mythologem through his song accompanied by the lyre; this was reserved for the male Orphic initiation. The image of a Silver Egg with a winged, creative god within was placed at the beginning of the world, which initiates experience in the forest on a full moon night.

The mythos was related in gesture, movement, and finally spoken word. This is the true meaning of the Greek word *mythos* – it is the ultimate revelation of the divine. The mythos is not a reenactment, but the divine event in regular reoccurrence. The myth and cult are one and the same. Mythos is cultus and cultus is mythos; they are inseparable.

"Lord, son of Leto, far shooter, mighty Phoibos, all-seeing, ruler over mortals and immortals, Helios, born aloft on golden wings, this is now the twelfth voice of those I heard from thee. 'Twas thou that said it, and thee thyself, far shooter, would I make my witness." (Orphic Fragment 62, Rhapsodic Theogony)

Thus Apollon is invoked as witness to the ensuing theogony.

At the beginning is Xrónos (Time), the ageless one. From Xrónos are born Aither, Khaos, and Erebos: the upper sky, the great yawning limitless gulf without bottom or foundation, and darkness over it all. Xrónos then fashions a great Silver Egg in the Aither.

After some time, the egg begins to rotate and then splits in two. The winged god Phanes, first-born (*Prōtogonos*) of the gods, appears. At the birth of Phanes, the misty gulf and Aither are rent apart.

Phanes is creator of the *Kosmos*. He is a beautiful figure of shining light with golden wings, four eyes, and the heads of various animals. He has the "voice of a bull and a glaring lion." He is of both sexes and bears within himself the seed of the gods. He has many names in the theogonies: Phanes, Prōtogonos, Phaiton, Erikepaios, Metis, Dionysos, Eros.

This first-born god makes an eternal home for the gods and becomes their first king. He fashions the sun and the moon. The men he creates are of the Golden Age. Phanes bears a daughter, Nyx (Night), who he takes as his partner. She assists him in creation.

Phanes passes the sceptre of rulership to "ambrosial" Nyx and gives her the gift of prophecy. Nyx gives her oracles from a cave to Adrasteia (also known as Ananke – "Necessity"), whose role is to make laws for the gods.

Nyx bears to Phanes two children: Gaîa and Ouranos (Earth and Heaven), who in turn produce the Titans (Kronos, Rhea, Okeanos, Tethys, etc.). The difference between the Orphic and standard versions is that there are seven male and seven female Titans, rather than the usual six and six.

Nyx hands supreme power over to her son Ouranos. Here, the common Greek Theogony takes place. Ouranos is mutilated by Kronos and Aphrodite is born from Ouranos' genitalia. Kronos becomes king of the gods and marries his sister Rhea. Because of a prophecy that tells of his downfall by his own children, Kronos swallows all his offspring as they are born.

Rhea tricks Kronos into swallowing a stone instead of his son Zeus, who is guarded by the Kouretes in a cave. Zeus releases the other gods from Kronos' stomach and together they overthrow the king of those "insolent" and "lawless" Titans, assisted by the Thunderbolt of Zeus that the Kyklopes fashioned for him. Only a few Titans are spared from being cast into Tartaros (deepest Underworld): in particular Okeanos, who refused to fight, and Rhea (mother of Zeus), who becomes Dēmḗtēr.

The divergent Orphic material takes up again at this point. Zeus swallows Phanes and takes into himself all that exists – the total *Kosmos*. He then recreates it, becoming creator and ruler of this era.

Orphic Fragment 167 states: *"Thus then engulfing the might of Erikepaios, the First-born, he held the body of all things in the hollow of his own belly; and he mingled with his own limbs the power and strength of the god. Therefore together with him all things in Zeus were created anew, the shining height of the broad Aither and the sky, the seat of the unharvested sea and the noble Earth, great Okeanos and the lowest depths beneath the Earth, and rivers and the boundless sea and*

47

all else, all immortal and blessed gods and goddesses, all that was then in being and all that was to come to pass, all was there, and mingled like streams in the belly of Zeus."

Gods old and new are all recreated and born of Zeus, the "father of gods and men." Nyx has a powerful position in all creations and each god destined to rule owes something to her care, as she is "nurse of the gods." All gods defer to her opinion, and in the era of Titans she cherishes Kronos most. She seems not to be swallowed up with the rest of the *Kosmos* as Zeus seeks the council of Nyx, holder of supreme wisdom and prophetic powers.

It is Nyx who unfolds the plan to trick Kronos and replace him with Zeus, who then humbly solicits Nyx for help in creating a new world. In *Orphic Fragment 165*, Zeus ponders how to establish his rule among gods and asks, *"How may I have all things one and each one separate?"*

Nyx answers, *"Surround all things with the ineffable Aither, and in the midst of that set the heaven, and in the midst of the boundless earth, in the midst the sea, and in the midst of all the constellations with which the heaven is crowned."* She goes on to say, *"Stretch a strong bond about all things, fitting a golden chain from the Aither."* (*Orphic Fragment 166*)

Zeus thus becomes "beginning, middle, and end of all." Athena, a brazen glory, springs from his head as the "dread accomplisher of the will of Kronos' son" and is given the name

Areté ("Excellence"). Zeus casts his seed into the sea and Aphrodite is born once again.

By Rhea (who has become Dēmétēr) he sires Kórē-Persephónē, the maiden destined to be ravished by Zeus and carried off by Pluto. Zeus sires Artemis-Hekátē and Apollon with Leto, then Apollon sires nine "grey-eyed" daughters with Persephónē. To Pluto Persephónē bears the Furies, to Zeus she bears Dionysos, "the sweet child of Zeus," the last to rule over the gods. Zeus hands power over to the infant, sets him on his throne with the sceptre, and tells the new gods that Dionysos is king.

The Titans, who found life again in Zeus' new world, are jealous of the infant and plot against him. The Titans distract Dionysos with a mirror then slay him, tearing him to pieces. His limbs are collected by Apollon on the orders of Zeus and taken to Delphoi. His heart is saved by Athena who brings it to Zeus so that Dionysos may be reborn. When the Titans kill the infant Dionysos they taste his flesh, incurring the wrath of Zeus. He throws his Thunderbolt and burns them up. From the smoking remnants arise the race of mortal men.

Dionysos is then reseeded into the womb of the mortal princess Semelē, who is tricked into asking Zeus to reveal his true form to her. She is immolated by lightning, but Zeus takes the unborn Dionysos and sews him into his thigh until he is ready to be born again.

Our nature is twofold as we are born from the Titans, the Wicked Sons of Earth, but there is also in us a heavenly nature, since some fragments of the body of Dionysos are too in us. The "immortal souls" of men are brought to the Underworld upon death by Hermês. The soul then enters different bodies in turn, cycling through animal and human lives until it can "cease from the circle and have respite from evil" following a set of moral and well-lived lives of purity.

"Many are the wand-bearers, but few are the Bakkhoi." (*Orphic Fragment 235*)

The *Orphic Theogony* is not meant to be analysed with reasoning and rationality. It is meant to convey powerful imagery to the initiate so he can gain realisation of the true nature of Being. That being said, some context and analysis is necessary for the contemporary seeker, as he has not had the preparation required to understand. This was the job of the initiator: the dark figure of Orpheus.

As Pindar states, Time is "father of all." Xrónos or Aion ("Eternity") is "ageless" and "great," and his "councils never perish." It is with Xrónos Agéraos ("Ageless Time") that all begins; he is cognate to the Iranian Zurvān Akarana ("Endless Time"). Time has always been and has always been a great power for both Good and Evil. An earlier depiction of Xrónos is as a serpent with wings, but by the time the theogonies are recorded he is stripped of these ancient attributes.

The image of the Winged Serpent wrapped around the Cosmic Egg is testimony to this more ancient form. The Cosmic Egg itself is found in the mythologies of India, Persia, Assyria, Egypt, Siberia, and Kamtschatka as well. It is deeply ancient and seems to be part of the mythos of cultures touched by Northern Hyperborean lore.

In the Theogony of Epimenídes the Kretan, Nyx produced the egg, while the Neoplatonists had no doubt that Xrónos did. Nyx may have preceded Xrónos in the earliest Theogonies. Regardless, from the egg is born Phanes.

Phanes derives from *phaínō* ("to shine"), because he shone forth in a blaze of light, illuminating all creation. He is called Protogonos ("First-born") as he is first of the gods to be created. This is also an epithet of Kórē-Persephónē. Embodying the creative principle, Phanes is called Eros ("Love") as well.

Phanes is also called Metis ("Counsel" or "Wisdom"), which is likewise name of the goddess Zeus swallows after hearing her child will be more powerful than he. Metis is the mother of Athena, but the battle goddess is born from Zeus' head after the "father of the gods" swallows Metis. This theme of being swallowed by Zeus is something that connects Phanes and Metis.

Another title of Phanes is Erikepaios. This is not Greek and there is no clear interpretation as to its meaning; it is sometimes also written as Irikepaigos. The name could denote "power."

The 6th century CE Byzantine chronicler Iōánnēs Malálas declared the names Metis, Phanes, Erikepaios to be "Counsel, Light, Life-giver." The Cult of Erikepaios is found also among the Lydian people, an Indo-European Anatolian group whose kingdom reached its maximum extent over Asia Minor in the 7th century BCE.

Phanes is a hermaphroditic composite, because he alone begins the process of creation. He is both "female and father." Phanes is an archetypal alchemical androgyne, like the Rebis or *res bina* ("double matter") of mediaeval alchemy.

The source of all is the Hyperborean Unity, which only an initiated seeker can attempt to return to through inner alchemical processes often signified with gynandrous symbolism. Rather than a physical manifestation of mundane sexual distinction, the hermaphrodite represents balancing polarised forces within the individual above illusory duality to a monistic Absolute. This typifies how gendered symbolism should be interpreted in a suprapersonal and metaphysical manner, beyond that of material human embodiment.

After Phanes hands over power to his daughter Nyx he retires, sitting in the recesses of the Cave of Night. Nyx sits in the middle of her cave making prophecies to the gods. Adrasteia is at the entrance to the cave, making laws for the gods by interpreting the mantic utterances of Nyx.

In Greek tradition the cave is always seat of the prophet. It is where deceased seers reside after being "swallowed by the earth." Amphiaraos, one of the Seven who fought against Thebes, was worshipped as a form of Zeus in a cave after his death. Odysseus goes to the cave mouth of the Underworld to consult the deceased seer Teiresias. The three ancient mantic beings who reside in a cave are echoed as the Graiai and Gorgons of the Perseus myth. These beings were reported to reside near the Hyperborean mountain by poet-seer Aristéas in his now lost *Arimaspea* poem.

The female channel of the voice of the gods is most prominently found in the mantis of the Delphic Oracle, the most ancient in Greece with a direct connection to Hyperborean tradition. She dwells in her "cave" giving visionary utterances that must be interpreted by the listener and put into action.

Nyx hands power to Ouranos, but continues to exert influence, giving advice to all rulers of the *Kosmos*. The gods regard her with awe. Despite deeply loving her grandson Kronos she nonetheless supports Zeus, since his is the rightful claim to rulership over the *Kosmos*.

The Titans are "lawless" as they flout the natural succession. Kronos refuses to give up the throne and war ensues for the first time. Kronos had begun the violence by castrating his father Ouranos at the instigation of Gaîa. Thus the peaceful Golden Age of Phanes gives way to the Silver and Bronze Ages.

The current *Kosmos* is that of Zeus. Zeus assimilates the principle of life, Eros, into himself when he swallows Phanes and the older *Kosmos*. He acquires creative power from the nature of Phanes. When Zeus swallows the *Kosmos*, he becomes "first-born" and "father of gods and men" as stated in the Epics. Zeus is Phanes because he swallows him, and Phanes is Dionysos because he is reborn from Zeus.

The Orphic tradition preserves an ancient Indo-European concept of gods dying and being reborn. All the Olympians and Titans are regenerated after Zeus swallows them and then recreates the *Kosmos*. This is also found in the Hindu and Buddhist traditions where gods live very long existences, then die and are reborn. The concept of a "second Aphrodite" is not unlike a reborn Śakra (Indra) of Buddhism.

Dionysos born in different forms is an idea not far removed from the avatars of Viṣṇu. Phanes is called Dionysos, so the god has existed since the creation of the gods. Hence he is one god, thrice born: Dionysos-Phanes, Dionysos-Zagreus (the Titans' victim), and Dionysos the resurrected.

Six generations of supreme governance are represented in the theogony: Phanes, Nyx, Ouranos, Kronos, Zeus, Dionysos. The *Kosmos* is absorbed and reissued by the divine powers, each overcoming the previous one. As the swallower, Zeus is a Wolf God: Zeus Lykaios ("Wolfish Zeus"). This Wolf God gives birth to the heroic principle of Aretē ("Excellence") embodied in the goddess Athena. She is the accomplisher of the will of Zeus, a brazen glory like an Iranian *Fravashi,* Germanic *Valkyrie,* or the inner *daímon* of the hero. Thus the Wolf Warrior initiate understands he lives in Zeus' wolfish world, and his blazing inner glory drives him towards excellence as his highest virtue.

The Zeus hymn of Pindar is lost to us, but known in part. In it, after he reorganises the *Kosmos,* Zeus asks the gods (who are lost in mute amazement) whether anything was still missing for perfection. They replied that just one thing was missing: a divine voice to proclaim and praise all this glory – and so they asked him to create the Muses. These Muses are ruled by Apollon, the voice of the *Kosmos,* which is channeled through the song of the initiator of the young wolves.

The Zeus *Kosmos* he sings of is not like that of Abrahamic religion, where a single god rules with an iron fist. As Walter Otto puts it in his work *Theophania:*

"This unity of the divine realm under Zeus, who as king and father subsumes everything in himself, is of a completely different kind than the monotheistic autocracy, which has only servants and agents around it. The individual deities, far from being mere organs of the supreme will, can indeed receive special orders from Zeus and may not act contrary to his plan; but they are and remain gods in the full sense, in whose eternity the universe with its forms of being is reflected. They are and remain the sublime representatives of the realms of the world and existence, the revelations of their divine depth, through which each of them is infinite and in its own way the whole of existence and the Godhead."

Ο Διόνυσος-Ζαγρεύς

Dionysos-Zagreus

The Orphic myth of Dionysos is connected to the Kretan cult mythos and links the god to another deity: Zagreus, a Chthonic Zeus. Thrakian god Sabazios is also linked to this same deity by both Graeco-Roman geographer Strabo and historian Diódōros Sikolos. Examining the myth and rites, transmission of the Dionysian myth can be traced back to the Indo-European mountain god cults of Asia Minor, with both a Southern Minoan and Northern Thrako-Phrygian linage that meet in the Orphic theogonic material.

The Orphic account of the death of Dionysos starts with Zeus impregnating his daughter Kórē-Persephónē. She gives birth to Dionysos on Krete and Zeus gives the child rulership of the *Kosmos*. Hera, angered by Zeus' infidelity and jealous of his son becoming king of the gods, incites the Titans to kill the infant.

Covered with gypsum and wearing masks of white earth, they surround the boy. With careful gestures they show the child fascinating toys: a top, a *rhombos* (bull roarer), dolls with jointed limbs, knucklebones, and a mirror. While the child Dionysos contemplates his own image in the circle of polished metal, the Titans strike.

The infant Dionysos attempts to escape the Titans by changing shape repeatedly, finally in the form of a bull. In this form he is eventually overcome. The Titans dismember him, and throw the pieces in the kettle.

They then roast them over the fire. They devour all except the heart – which had been divided into equal parts – before Zeus strikes them down with lightning, reducing them to ashes from whence men are born. Athena brings the heart to Zeus who swallows it. Zeus then impregnates Semelē with the "New Dionysos." After the fiery death of Semelē, Zeus carries the infant to term in his thigh as Dionysos Eiraphiotes ("sewn in" Dionysos). Thus Dionysos is born from his father.

This new Dionysos is a form of the deity known to exoteric Greek religion. He is the god who dresses in women's clothing and is attended by Mainades, wild women who nurse and then dismember animals in remembrance of his ordeal. He is god of ecstatic communion with divinity through dance, drama, and intoxication.

A god in the form of a child is jointly slaughtered by all the Titans: "kings of ancient times." This, like the later Dionysiac rending of animals is a manifestation of the bull sacrifice as performed on Krete. In his Kretan cult, centred on the sacred cave on Mount Ida, Dionysos-Zagreus was consumed as an initiatic sacrament in the form of a bull, whose flesh was eaten raw.

The Kretan rite was known as the *Omophagia* ("eating of raw flesh"). The worshippers carried a *kista* (casket) as the receptacle of the heart of Dionysos during the Rites. A snake – the spirit of the earth and fertility – then issued from the mystic chest of Dionysos, representing the god's rebirth from the heart.

The Kretan mystery god was originally called Zagreus, "God of Mount Zagron" the "Great Hunter." The Akhaian Greeks associated this god with Zeus upon their invasion of Krete, naming him Zeus Khthónios ("Chthonian Zeus"). This was common among the Greeks in naming cave deities, such as Zeus Trophonios and Zeus Amphiaraos – both of whom were soothsayers rendered into subterranean existence as full gods. Also known as Idean Zeus, this mountain cave god then took on the name of the Thrakian god Dionysos (also known in Thraki as Sabazios) after the deity travelled down through Greece from the north.

The Northern Religion merged with these Kretan rites and god. This was because they were of the same origin, beyond the Phrygian homeland in the Zagros mountains (between Iran and Iraq), home to the Kassites, Guti, Elamites, and Mitanni. All remain unclassified apart from the Mitanni, who were Indo-European people.

The Thakian god Sabazios is related to the Lunar Bull. He is the sky father and horseman god of the Phrygians and Thrakians. Normally depicted on horseback with his staff of power, Sabazios' horse places his hoof on the head of the Lunar Bull.

Later this rider god is explicitly associated with Zeus. He is also mentioned alongside Mercury by the Romans, who believed Sabazios to be both Dionysos and Apollon. On this Macrobius writes, *"Liber and Helios (Dionysos and Apollon) are worshipped by the Thakians as Sabazios."*

While Sabazios seems not to have much to do with either god, his worship and imagery clearly have a Dionysian connection. Initiates of his cult are purified with white clay, like the gypsum worn by the Titans when they rend Dionysos.

Sabazios is usually depicted as a right hand in the *benedictio Latina* gesture affixed to a sceptre. On the thumb is a pinecone. A serpent (or pair of serpents) encircles the wrist and surmounts the bent ring and pinky fingers, like the snakes on the Samothrákian Mysteries' dual columns. A lightning bolt over the index and middle fingers denotes the thunderbolt of Zeus.

More evidence of the dual route transmission lies in the names used in the cult and myth. Bakkhos, the cult name of Dionysos derives from Baki, a Lydian name that came on the Southern Indo-European route. Semelē, the second mother of Dionysos *Dimḗtēr* ("of two mothers"), is derived from Zemele, the Thrako-Phrygian "Earth Mother." This comes from the Northern route. Semelē is the youngest daughter of the founder of Thebes, Kadmos, who was worshipped as part of the secret ritual of the Samothrákian mysteries.

Both Kórē, the first mother of Dionysos, and Semelē are earth goddesses, but in a distinctly Greek manner, no importance is given to the Mother, or the Virgin goddesses in the worship of Dionysos. The only element that remained of the mother was the frenzy of the Thyiades ("awakeners") and Mainades ("dismemberers"). In myth, Dionysos resurrects his mother Semelē as a goddess Thyōnē who, as her name suggests, "inspires frenzy."

There were three key elements to the Kretan Ritual: carrying the Serpent emblem of the chthonian god, slaying and eating the bull, and the war dance of the young warriors. Known as the dance of the Kouretes, it involved clashing weapons and was part of the warrior initiation ritual associated with the Kretan cave rites. In myth, the Kouretes – a circle of friendly *daimónes* – dance around the infant Zeus on Mount Ida to keep his presence hidden from Kronos. He who performed the Kretan ritual dance became a new Koures. The god of the cave was addressed as *Kouros* ("Youth") by the initiates.

The Korybantes are a Northern Anatolian equivalent who in Greece became associated with Apollon. In Anatolia, they were originally related to the Phrygian Great Mother Kybele-Rhea, who in Greece was the mother of Zeus. The Korybantes were also ecstatic attendant *daímones*, very similar to the Kouretes of Krete who became allied to Dionysos. The Kabeiroi of Samothráki and Thebes are also related.

In Theban Boetia, there is evidence of Kábeiros (singular of Kábeiroi) being worshipped next to Pais ("child"). Kabeiros is portrayed like Dionysos. The Scholiast to Apollŏnios Rhódios says: *"Others say that there were once two Kábeiroi, the elder Zeus, the younger Dionysos."* On Samothráki, two Kábeiroi were worshipped in the mysteries. Among the archaeological finds of Kábeiran worship in Thebes are spinning tops and knuckle bones: the Playthings of Dionysos as votive offerings to the divine child.

The playthings the Titans used to lure Dionysos include the *konos* (pine cone) and *rhombos* (bull roarer). The *konos* was what topped the *thyrsos* (wand) carried during Dionysian rites. The *rhombos* was the bull roarer used by the Korybantes. Both were considered "spinning tops" – the toys of a child. These playthings, along with other ritual items were kept in the *cistae mysticae* ("mystic casket") of the Roman Orphic-Dionysian mysteries.

Of these playthings, it is the mirror which finally captivates the infant Dionysos. He looks at his reflection and sees the opposition of the eternal intelligible world and the unreal world of birth and decay, foreshadowing of the dual nature of man who is born of his remains. The Titans also distract him with the golden apples of the Hesperides, a symbol of immortality.

The rending of Dionysos Sparagmós ("torn to pieces" Dionysos) and boiling him in milk is clearly linked to immortality. It is a rite harkening back to human sacrifice, which had long disappeared from Greek religion. All meat comes from sacrificial killing.

In ancient sacrificial cooking, viscera are cooked over the sacred fire while larger pieces are boiled. In Krete the sheep raiders in Sphakia still boil the meat from a stolen animal rather than roasting it. The theft and boiling of meat is a living reflex of the Kretan Dionysos-Zagreus cult.

A kid boiled in milk is part of secret ritual, as the "Orphic" golden lamellae (magic scrolls worn by the dead) attest to with their inscriptions, such as *"I am a kid fallen into milk,"* and *"Welcome, thou who hast suffered such suffering as thou hadst never before suffered. From man thou hast become become a god; a kid, thou hast fallen into milk!"*

These gold foil grave goods were intended as Underworld "passports" of a kind. The tale of the god born again from a cauldron of milk after being dismembered is reflected in another myth. Médeia, wife of Iásōn, tricks his wicked uncle Pelias by killing, chopping up, and cooking an old goat in a cauldron, then resurrecting it as a kid. She then does not resurrect Pelias when chopped up by his own daughters. The milk is the mother's milk, which nurtures the newborn immortal child.

Sacrifice in the Indo-European mythos is intended to remake the whole that has been torn asunder. This is particularly the case in Vedic myth and ritual. In the Vedic creation myth Prajāpati rapes his daughter Uṣás, but Rudra fires his arrow and spills the seed of Prajāpati, thereby creating a multiplicity from the original unity of Brahman.

In the Indo-Iranian Avesta, primordial man and king Gayō Marətan (whose name translates to "Mortal Life") is sacrificed and dismembered by the Daēvas. These are the Iranian equivalent of Titans. They likewise create a multitude from unity.

In the Orphic tradition, Zeus too rapes his daughter Kórē producing Zagreus-Dionysos. Similarly, the Titans are primaeval renderers. They analogously dismember the One (Dionysos) into multiplicity.

Divinity is then divided among men by Zeus throwing his thunderbolt. After the division of original unity into manifold creation, Dionysos (the One) is born again from Zeus. He is incomplete however, as the souls of men carry part of him within.

Dionysos is *bios*, the world soul, like Vedic brahman. Prajāpati is Prōtogonos; Phanes, the cosmic proto-Dionysos. His other name is Eros (Love), since it implies attraction – the mixing of elements to create forms. Vedic Kama (Love) is also linked with Rudra-Śiva.

Indo-European roots lie at the heart of both sets of myth and ritual. The Orphic tradition sets Dionysos in his rightful place as *bios*: the divine spark of Aither within man. The aim of an Orphic was to purge the Titanic (earthly) element and exalt the Dionysiac (celestial). Denoting this mix within man is the Orphic statement: *"I am a child of Earth and starry Heaven; but my race is of Heaven (alone)."*

The Titans are children of Ouranos and Gaîa, while Dionysos is of Zeus and the earth goddess. Both are offspring of heaven and earth, so man too contains that mix. The Orphics sacrificed to Dionysos "in all seasons of the year" so they could free themselves of their "lawless ancestry."

Dionysos is called "Liberator" because he represents the celestial element within the earthly. In order to purify himself, man must perform the self-sacrifice, being rid of his Titanic nature through asceticism and ritual. The Orphics believed reincarnation allowed for many opportunities to accomplish this spiritual purification.

η Ὀρφικὴ Ψυχή

The Orphic Soul

The Orphic conception of *psykhḗ* ("soul") is bound in terms of Titanic and Dionysiac elements. As men are formed from both, the aim of an Orphic mystic is to separate divine from earthly, ascending to a godlike state of immortality. The soul lives on, according to Pindar *"since this alone is derived from the gods"* (*Fragment 131*).

The *psykhḗ* goes through the cycle of generation and is reincarnated in various forms after passing through judgement in the Underworld. This is a teaching that Plato took from the Orphics: *"We must ever maintain a real belief in the ancient and sacred stories, which reveal that our soul is immortal, and has judges, and pays the utmost penalties whenever a man is rid of the body."* (Plato, *7ᵗʰ letter 335a*)

The journey of the soul starts with it floating in the Aither. Carried from it by the winds, it is breathed in by the newly-born life form. Mythologically, this is a motif found in the creation of the "wind-born" cosmic egg.

From the egg hatched Phanes who brought the world from night to light. This motif was originally reserved for the male Orphic initiation: the theogonic image of the Silver Egg, conceived by Wind and Night, with a winged, creative god within. These initiates experienced this beginning of the world while in the forest on a full moon night.

The alternative theogony where Nyx bore the egg to the wind is found in the *Birds* of Aristophanes who reproduces the version by Epimenídes of Krete. He has his birds say:

"In the beginning there existed only Chaos, Night, Black Erebos and Dreary Tartaros: there was no Earth, no Air, no Sky. It was in the boundless womb of Erebos that the first egg was laid by black-winged Night; and from this egg, in due season, sprang Eros the deeply-desired, Eros the bright, the golden-winged. And it was he, mingling in Tartaros with murky Chaos, who begot our race and hatched us out and led us up to the light. There was no race of immortal gods till Eros brought the elements together with love: only then did the Sky, the Ocean, and the Earth come into being, and the deathless race of all the blessed gods." (Aristophanes, *The Birds* 685)

Aristophanes calls the egg "wind-born." This has a second meaning in Greek: an egg born of the hen alone with no father. The god Hephaistos is the "wind-child" of Hera, for example. The Egg was laid by Nyx alone without a father. But this also encodes the concept of the soul, or life principle being air, borne on the winds and drawn into the body at birth.

Psykhē means both breath and soul, like the Latin *anima*. This concept originates in the Orphic tradition and then develops throughout Classical thought. It is for this reason that the *Tritopátores* ("thrice-ancestors"), benevolent Attic wind spirits, were invoked at wedding celebrations in Athens. The Byzantine *Soûda* calls them the "doorkeepers and guardians of the winds," thereby making them the responsible for the rebirth of the soul. These ancestral wind spirits are similar to the Vedic *Maruts*, wind spirits who bring fecundity through the rains, and the Avestan *Fravaṣis* who are associated with the divine Spirit within man.

Once a divine spark is born in a human body, its onward journey depends on one's actions. The *kyklos genéseos* ("cycle of generation"), or "circle of necessity," binds the soul. This reincarnation sends a soul through many existences; it is represented physically in wheels found in the temples of Persephónē, but also those of Hekátē and Apollon. The Orphic aimed to exult and purify through ascesis his Dionysiac nature in order to shake off the earthly self and fulfil his potential to become immortal and divine. He understood the source of distress lay in the body's appetites and passions, much like the Buddhist concept of *duḥkha* ("suffering"). He strove to subdue that Titanic element, "fly out of the weary wheel," and "attain the heights;" or as *Fragment 226* of Proklos states: *"To escape from the circle and havè a respite from misery."* This was expressed in the semantic device of a body (*soma*) being the soul's tomb (*sema*).

The early Orphics believed in the "thrice ancient law" of *"what thou hast done thou shalt suffer."* This karmic concept holds a man's actions in life, which is a trial, determine his punishment in Hāídēs and subsequent rebirth. A life of *adikía* ("injustice") stifles the divine element and the Titanic element dominates. This is *"the unreasonable and disorderly and violent part of us"* as Plutarch states in *On the Eating of Flesh (996c)*. To misuse the divine spark within is to secure one's place in the dark underworld.

Later Orphism broke away from the doctrine of self-reliance and made the releasing gods the only vehicle of salvation – a degeneration of its original ideas. They believed the uninitiated would "lie in mud" in Hāídēs, whereas the purified would live with the gods. This is based on an older passage of the soul of a departed through the Underworld, which came to dominate later Orphism as the main concern rather than being just part of the journey. Initiation into the mysteries of an Underworld passage became the only important part of a Dionysian Orphic cult. To become *kekatharménos* ("one who has been purified") and *tetelesménos* ("one who has been initiated into the Mysteries") was the only requirement for liberation, as one could understand the Underworld journey and navigate it correctly.

We know much of this journey through the Underworld thanks to Plato (particularly his *Phaido* and *Pʰaidros*), but also from the Bakkhic-Orphic gold plates, or *lamellai* of the 4ᵗʰ century BCE found in Krete and Southern Italy. Worn around the neck of deceased initiates, these golden scrolls were inscribed with verses from Orphic teachings and acted as *totenpässe*: passports for the dead.

These gold plates give instructions on what to do upon reaching the Underworld – the way to go and words to say. They contain similar information to the Tibetan *Bardo Thodol* or Egyptian *Book of the Dead*. According to the *Axiokhos* traditionally attributed to Plato, the lot of a soul in Hãidēs was the subject of writing on bronze tablets brought by two seers to the island of Delos from the Hyperboreans.

Upon reaching the Underworld, the soul must pass through a barrier of mud. Those who get stuck in the overflowing "filth" breached morality in life: wronged a stranger, robbed a child, struck a parent, committed perjury. They are punished with "burial in filth" due to their Titanic impurity. The soul is judged and punished if it has committed impure acts in life. For example, endlessly carrying water in a leaky *pithos* (jar) to fill a bottomless container is a punishment for those who lived a life of immorality or of never being satisfied, as carnal desire never fulfils the soul.

It is through this punishment that Persephónē receives requital from the soul for "ancient doom" – the killing of Dionysos by the Titans. It is therefore the Titanic element which is punished, thereby cleansing the soul in order that it may be reborn in a clean state. This is not an allusion to individual sin, but the Titanic nature of man. In life, the individual must purify his Spirit through heroic striving, not through piety towards a god.

According to Pindar, after nine years in Hãȋdēs, Persephónē gives the souls back to the sun above. In order to return to the upper world of the living, the soul must travel the path through the Underworld. It is this route that is prescribed by the gold plates. According to Plato, there is a fork in the Asphodel Meadows of the Underworld. The upward, righthand path leads to the Isles of the Blessed; the downward, lefthand path leads to Tartaros, the "Great Gulf." The navigation of this route is critical to the reincarnation of the Spirit. It is at this juncture that the Spirit must make a choice between forgetfulness or remembering.

The 4th century BCE gold plate from Petelia gives the following instructions:

"Thou shalt find to the left of the House of Hãȋdēs a spring,
And by the side thereof standing a white cypress.
To this spring approach not near.
But thou shalt find another, from the Lake of Memory
Cold water flowing forth, and there are guardians before it.
Say, 'I am a child of Earth and starry Heaven;
But my race is of Heaven (alone). This ye know yourselves.
But I am parched with thirst and I perish. Give me quickly
The cold water flowing forth from the Lake of Memory.'
And of themselves they will give thee to drink of the holy spring.
And thereafter among the other heroes thou shalt have lordship."

This tells of the route and words to say. The Spirit travels on the path on the right over the Plain of Lethe ("forgetfulness"), and at the end is parched with thirst. Proving it is pure, it may drink from the Lake of Memory, escaping the cycle of birth as a divinity. The Spirit is then "adopted" into the family of gods by Persephónē-Kórē, bestower of immortality.

The soul is a child of Earth and Heaven as the Titans are born of Gaîa and Ouranos. The Spirit's race is of Heaven alone, since it is of Dionysos and has kinship with gods. It is the immortal Spirit that is instructed to say these words. Humans are composite; due to their Titanic element men are prone to dark acts, but also have a divine part that can be purified and ascend to immortality.

After death, the soul is judged in Hāîdēs and given time in the Underworld. It is then born again into the cycle of birth; however the noble and initiated may choose their next life. Free will and personal responsibility are essential elements of original Orphic thought.

When the Spirit has atoned for its actions of its last life, it is permitted by the Underworld deities to be reborn. The Spirit then drinks from the water of Lethe to forget all but dim recollections of what it has learned over its previous life. The fully purified Spirit does not drink of the waters of Lethe at all, while the ignorant drink fully and the wise only a little.

Learning in this life is no more than recollection, as the soul has on its age-long path through earthly and otherworldly existences caught glimpses of the true reality, which is immaterial. The Spirit has seen everything, but reincarnation has made it forget and it simply needs to be reminded. This is called *Anamnesis* ("unforgetting"): the remembering of all a Spirit knew before its current life.

The initiate understands the fall of the Spirit and its ascent back to its place of divinity, as mentioned in a fragment of the *Katharmoi* of Empedokles. Some believed every third incarnation was as a man and that three incarnations as a man led to the possibility of liberation; that three pure and holy lives in succession could lead to release. Pindar echoes this, saying the soul is "the image of life" – a spiritual double that must live three faultless lives to escape the material plane. Purity determines the next life.

The Orphics knew of four states of being for the Spirit. The infernal is Tartaros, where the wicked reside for punishment. Elysion, or the Isles of the Blessed, is a paradise where the noble can enjoy godlike pleasures. The Cycle of Generation is the earthly circle of lives. Finally, they knew release: the permanent and true divine state of Spirit.

Aside from liberation all states of being are temporary. The Isles of the Blessed are a final immortal place for heroes in exoteric Greek religion. In the esoteric Orphic strain, this is just a temporary Underworldly state that must be overcome.

Plato regarded this as a trial that may make the Spirit careless in choosing its next life. This is like the Buddhist concept of a *deva* state, leading to accumulation of further karma and a slip into a lower rebirth. Elysion is "on the farthest borders of the Earth," but still a sublunar realm like Tartaros.

According to Aristotle, *air* is a semi-pure atmosphere between earth and moon. The moon is a resting place for souls, and when destined for rebirth they occupy levels of *air*. The soul draws new life in with the *air* at birth. It *"comes into us from space as we breathe, borne by the wind."* (Aristotle, *On the Soul* 1.5.4)

Divinity dwells in the *Aither*, which fills the outer reaches of Heaven. *Aither* itself is divine: it is both the dwelling of Zeus and Zeus himself. The divine spark, the Spirit, is a spark of *Aither*.

As the stars are made of *Aither*, the Orphics believed the immortal Spirit became a star in the Milky Way: the "abode of souls." They believed stars to be habitable worlds in the infinite *Aither*. Plato states each Spirit has a star and returns to dwell there after transcending the cycle.

In order to achieve this, the initiate must become a *Bakkhos*: a sacred, purified person with magical powers. This is a rare state to achieve, as Olympiodoros states, *"Many are the wand-bearers, but few the Bakkhoi"* (*Orphic Fragment 235*). A person who has achieved this state is called *Bakkhos*, a title of Dionysos.

Dionysos represents the divine spark. He is "mad" or "wild" to human senses, as mortals are not able to witness the pure gods in their true manifestations. Dionysos is ecstatic; he is the pure ecstasy allowing for rapture. This is the passing from human to immortal form.

When the Queen of the Underworld considers a soul's "ancient guilt" as atoned for, she sends it forth to the upper world to live a final life as a king, wise man, or man of valour. He becomes *Bakkhos*, and upon death surpasses the material world.

The Spirit that has its final human incarnation goes to Elysion with those destined for rebirth. Travelling on the "Way of Zeus," it lives for a while with the great ones under protection of Kronos in his "Citadel" on the Isles of the Blessed. From there, it flies up to the higher sphere of *Pure Aither*.

The Spirit soars upward from earthly and lunar planes. It has risen out of its material tomb and is born on the immaterial. Free, it now truly begins to live in "the unbroken radiance of divinity." *Aither* is the god-like form equivalent to Indic *deva*, while *Pure Aither* is a state of *metátheos-atideva*: beyond the gods in pure divinity.

το ταξίδι της Αργούς

Voyage of The Argo – The Initiation

In *Undying Glory: The Solar Path of Greek Heroes*, the story of Iásōn and the Argonauts was examined for its Solar messaging. As with all myth, there are deep layers of meaning that have been laminated together over time. The tale of the voyage of the Argo and Iásōn is one of the oldest with several iterations.

The most famous is the third century BCE Hellenistic rendering of the myth by Apollōnios Rhódios. However, there is evidence (in the story itself and the artistic record) of parallel versions of the tale, and a pre-Iliadic Iásōn and his journey to obtain the Golden Fleece. Pindar and Euripides both deal with elements of the Iásōn myth, and there is a late *"Orphic Argonautika"* that has Orpheus as hero of the tale.

While the Orphic version is a later rendering, it does belie an Orphic element in narratives passed down from high antiquity. Orpheus is one of the Argonauts in all accounts. When considering Orpheus' role as initiator into the Wolf Cult, the journey begins to come into focus as an initiation itself.

Orpheus is the first Argonaut mentioned in Apollṓnios Rhódios' rendering. It says how he charmed the oaks to the Thrakian shore. This sets the story's mood as a magical initiatic experience. Shortly after Orpheus in the list of Argonauts is Ankaîos. As Apollṓnios puts it: *"So there went Ankaîos, dressed in a local bearskin, and swinging an enormous two-edged axe in one hand."* Ankaîos is son of Lykourgos ("Wolf-worker"). Hailing from Arkadía ("Bear Land"), he wears a black bear skin and wields an axe, invoking berserker-like symbolism. He represents the wolf initiate: a Northern man of deep antiquity. According to Apollṓnios, the Arkadians were the first people to settle in Greece.

The Argonauts are sons of gods and heroes. They assemble to voyage to Kolkhís and retrieve the Golden token of their journey. This is an Underworld initiatic experience.

From the very outset there is a dispute among the heroes. To settle it, Orpheus sings a song of the creation of the *Kosmos*. He tells how "All was One" and that Ophíon ("Serpent") and Eurynomé ("Wide-ruling") ruled Olympus before Kronos and Rhea. This is the *Orphic Theogony*.

The Argonauts first land on Samothráki, *"the island of Atlas' daughter Ēléktrā,"* at Orpheus' request and are initiated into the Mysteries there. Iásōn (or Iasíōn) is possibly derived from

Ēetíōn, one of the oldest names of one of the gods on the island. Ēetíōn was son of Zeus and Ēléktrā, and the island was also called Ēléktris, implying electricity and the sun.

The Samothrákian Mysteries (treated later in this book) were ancient Thrakian mysteries linked to the Orphic initiatic transmission. Thus, the Argonauts are all given initiation into the Wolf Cult before entering the Underworld for an excursion to retrieve Golden Light from darkness. With Orpheus as guide, this begins their passage through the land of the dead to that of the rising sun. At the end of this journey is rebirth.

The *"Argo sailed onward, sped by Thrakian winds,"* the Apollonian Wolf Winds harnessed by the initiates. They arrive in the land of the Doliones and are welcomed by their king Kyzikós *"after ascertaining their race and mission."* The Doliones are Phrygians and claim Poseidon as ancestor. Poseidon means "Lord of the Earth" and is the Earth God of a Pre-Olympian pantheon who is married to an Earth Goddess. The Olympian Sea God retains this previous aspect as "Earth Shaker" and god of horses.

After accidentally killing Kyzikós, Iásōn has to propitiate the "Mother of the Gods" at her mountain shrine on Dindymon. This is the Phrygian Mountain Mother Kybele known to the Greeks as Rhea, "Mistress of Many Names," the Earth Goddess. Iásōn and his men row on to the "Thrakian Harbour" to climb the mountain island – a reflection of the Hyperborean Mountain of initiation. On the top, Iásōn carves a sacred image of the

"Mountain Goddess" from an ancient vine stump. This *xoanon* image of the goddess is carved from the Dionysian vine: another initiatic clue.

He then places the image under the shade of the topmost oaks, heaps a gravel altar and adorns it with garlands of oak leaves. This is his symbolic tomb: a hero's grave adorned with the oak of Zeus. He dedicates it to Dindyméné the Mother, Lady of Many Names, the Earth Goddess who frees souls from the Underworld. Apollodoros says "from that day the Phrygians have worshipped Rhea with bull-roarer and kettledrum." The mountain is called "Bear Mountain," revealing the goddess in her aspect as Hyperborean gatekeeper Artemis. At Orpheus' command the men do a war dance in full armour, beating their shields like the Korybantes

They next come to Mount Arganthónios, which is explicitly sacred to Artemis. Here, pulled into a spring by a nymph is Hylas, a man lost to the lures of a blissful Underworld existence due to not liberating himself by completing the Wolf Initiation. The wolf theme is made explicit after the Argonauts encounter the Bebrykians and their king Amykos, who is defeated in a boxing match by Polydeukes. Upon the death of the king, a battle ensues.

"As on a day in winter the grey wolves, coming down, will panic the countless flocks in the sheepfolds, undetected by the sheepdogs' keen noses or even by the shepherds, and go looking for what they can first jump and carry off, eyeing the whole mass at once, and the sheep run

huddling together, tumbling over each other; so these heroes spread fearful panic among the high-riding Bebrykians." (Apollónios Rhódios, *Argonautika* 2.123-129)

Following this, Orpheus leads the song during sacrifice and feast as his role demands.

The next scene is also a stage of initiation with overt Hyperborean overtones. The Argonauts find Phineús, blind seer of Apollon, being tormented by the Harpies (half bird women). Phineús was king of the Thrakians before Zeus punished him with blindness for revealing too much to mortals.

The Harpies come and eat all the food that is given him whenever it is time to eat, leaving only their excrement and food scraps. Phineús swears an oath on the "Underworld gods" that Zètes and Kalaïs, sons of Boreas the North Wind, will not incur the wrath of Heaven for helping him.

The gods are those who swear oaths on the River Styx. Men swear by touching the Earth like Rhea when she gave birth to Zeus. The oaths of both gods and men are sworn on infernal powers: primal forces with the ability to affect fate.

Zeus gives the Boreads (Zètes and Kalaïs) power to chase the Harpies. They take flight and almost catch the "Hounds of Zeus." Before they can, the goddess Iris stops them and swears they will leave Phineús alone, making an oath on the River Styx.

The Harpies' lair is on Mount Dikte on "Minoan Krete." The Harpies are spirits of the hot Southern wind bringing pestilence and blight. The Boreadai are spirits of the North Wind: the cooling, deathly wind associated with both Hyperborea and wolves during the summer months. Thus the pestilential Harpies foul the food of Phineús, but are chased away by the clean, clear Northern Wolf Winds.

Phineús gives the Argonauts directions they need, like a key to a map, and then prays, *"May the gods grant me a quick death; after dying I'll have my share, then, of all that delights the heart."* This is an Orphic conception of death marking a transition into the Underworld portion of an initiatic journey. They pass through the Clashing Rocks and cross the mouth of the Akhéron (an Underworld river), then by the cape of Karambis facing the "ever-circling bear" (the constellation is a Hyperborean symbol). Above the cape "the blasts of the North wind are split asunder." All these markers are a map of Return.

In the Eúxeinos Póntos (Black Sea) they land on the deserted island of Thynias. Before dawn, an impalpable glimmer suffuses the night. This is the *lykóphos* or predawn "wolf light." At this moment, they see Apollon travelling from Lykia to Hyperborea. True to form Orpheus is first to speak, naming the island "the holy island of Dawntime Apollon."

This segment of the story is a clear reference to the Wolf Cult initiation. The Argonauts build an altar, offering burnt fat, thigh bones, and libations. An altar of loose stones is raised and the men hunt fawns and wild goats for sacrifice in the manner of *ephēboi* youths in the wilderness during their rite of passage before completing initiation.

Orpheus states *"be gracious, O Lord, be gracious, who wert manifest unto us."* This is a revealing line and seems like something that would be stated by an initiator during a shamanic visionary experience. Apollon's locks are forever unshorn; he is inviolate – an eternal youthful god of the Wolf Cult. This is ancient Orphic Wolf Cultism where meat is not prohibited and sacrifice is employed. The Argonauts dance and offer prayer shouting out *"Ié Paion!"* ("Shoot it Apollon!"), the cultic cry of the god.

Two of the Argonauts, Idmon and Tiphys, die at the Akhéron River, so Ankaîos takes over helmsman duty from Tiphys; thus the bearskin-wearing axe warrior of the North becomes man at the helm. The consummate Wolf Cult warrior steers the ship for the rest of the journey, the ship reaching Fairdance River where Dionysos held secret rites before a cavern called "the Lodge" on his way back from India. Here they see the tomb of Sthénelos and his ghost who is released briefly by Persephóné: a reminder of the Orphic conception of soul. The Maiden is a goddess able to release a shade from its time in the Underworld. They stop and make offerings to the dead hero and raise another altar to Apollon; Orpheus dedicates his lyre on the altar. The Argonauts then sail past the river Parthenios ("of the maiden/virgin"), which is sacred to Artemis who in Orphic thought is conflated with Kórē-Persephóné.

They arrive at Kolkhís and one of the first things we learn is that Kolkhians do not bury or cremate their male dead. They hang them in an ox hide from a tree. The giant Orion is born from an ox hide in Greek myth; in the ancient Kretan rites of Dionysos an ox hide is a vessel of rebirth and transformation, as it is where honey is turned into mead. This later became wine stored in the wineskin.

Other small pieces of information are hidden in the text at this point too, such as the purple robe Hypsípylé gave to Iásōn was made for Dionysos. Purple is the colour of the fillet worn by Samothrákian initiates. We also learn that the Keltoi (Celts) sing that the amber floating on the Eridanos River is from when Apollon was banished by Zeus from Heaven to the land of the Hyperboreans; thus amber is Apollon's tears.

It is also stated Médeia (an enchantress who out of love helps Iásōn) will become wife of Akhilleús in Elysion. This is an Orphic belief. In Apollónios' telling she helps Iásōn perform a magic rite to the goddess Hekátē before enduring the trial of sowing a dragon's teeth for her father King Aiétēs.

Médeia then takes Iásōn to the sacred grove of Ares and lulls the serpent to sleep so Iásōn can take the fleece. This is a clear retelling of the Dragonslayer myth where the Wolf Cult hero slays the dragon to gain a boon or prize. In this case it is the ram's pelt or "fleece of Zeus."

This is the "purifying fleece" used to cleanse those tainted with blood before they can be initiated. It is the "medicine" with power to purify, and if slept on can furnish a divine dream. A ram's fleece was worn by *ephēboi* in the cave of Zeus Akraios (or the Kheironion) during their initiation on Mount Pelion. This fleece is also a substitute for a wolf's pelt, as the wolf and flocks are intimately connected.

The Argonauts must make their way back to the land of living to complete their initiation. They sail back with several trials while pursued by the Kolkhians. Iásōn slays Médeia's brother Apsyrtos on Artemis' sanctuary, requiring him to be purified by the sorceress Kírkē (aunt of Médeia). This is an infernal human sacrifice to the goddess Hekátē, who – as we will see in the *Orphic Argonautika* – is recognised as being the same goddess as Artemis.

The Argonauts pass the Sirens, and we learn they were originally attendants of Persephónē before she was abducted. This once more weaves into the story the Queen of the Underworld. The Argonauts successfully pass the Sirens, because Orpheus plays his lyre to drown out their song.

Among the Phaiakians, Iásōn and Médeia are married in the Cave of Makris. Makris was the nursemaid of Dionysos who smeared the god's lips with honey when Hermês rescued him from the fire that killed his second mother Semelē. This is another Orphic clue in the text.

Towards the end of their journey, they arrive at the tree of the Hesperides a day after Herakles slew the serpent Ladon and stole the apples. In the story the wedding attendants mourn the death of the second serpent in a tree. These are the two pillars with serpents entwined, each on either side of the world. Twin serpents and pillars feature in the initiation at Samothráki.

Charmed by Orpheus, the Hesperides tell the Argonauts of a spring at Triton's lake from which they can escape the Libyan desert. This is the Underworld spring at the Lake of Memory. The desert is the Plain of Lethe: the place the Argonauts complete their initiation, which parallels the Orphic soul's transformation into Divinity. It is at the lake Orpheus declares they should give Apollon's tripod to the local deities.

The *Argonautika* of Apollónios Rhódios hides an initiatic map. The keys to the map are only truly known by an Orphic initiate. We must do our best to recognise these clues to the journey of Hyperborean ascent when we encounter them in our own voyage North.

The *Orphic Argonautika* is a much later version, written at least 700 years after Apollónios Rhódios composed his telling. In this version Orpheus takes centre stage and is a driving force of the narrative. There are ancient elements, but it has a clear late Orphic mytheme. There was once an older *Orphic Argonautika* in the Orphic *Rhapsodies*; the author of the surviving *Orphic Argonautika* saw the Orphic threads in the ancient myth, emphasised, and embellished them.

Orpheus strokes "winged serpents," he has a contest of song with Kheírōn winning a Dionysiac leopard skin from the kentaur, and Eros is called "the most ancient one." They also go to Samothráki to perform the Mysteries at the bidding of Orpheus, who also charms the Clashing Rocks to stay open. The story has a much quicker pace and is considerably shorter than Apollṓnios' version, but has many of the same major points.

The real difference is in how the Fleece is obtained at Kolkhís. The Golden Fleece is kept in a sacred grove protected by a statue of "Artemis of the gate," who is Hekátē. The plants within the sacred grove such as asphodel are Underworldly, poisonous, and medicinal. The Fleece is hanging on an oak and guarded by a golden serpent that also guards the tomb of Zeus Khamaizelos ("zealous for the ground") – Chthonian Zeus.

With the help of Mḗdeia, Orpheus performs an infernal ritual, praying to the furies. This ritual causes the goddesses Pandóra and Hekátē to appear. Pandóra has a body of iron while Hekátē has the heads of a horse, dog, and lion. Pandóra is another incarnation of the earth mother as her name means "all-giving." The statue of "Artemis" relaxes and the gate to the grove opens. Orpheus lulls the serpent to sleep so Iásōn can take the Fleece.

The Argo then sails "North" where they observe several tribes including the Arimaspi, who were neighbours of the Hyperboreans. Another tribe they pass are the "Arktai." They fall into Okeanos, which the Hyperborean men call the Kronion Sea or Dead Sea (Arctic Ocean). The Sirens kill themselves upon hearing Orpheus' song in the *Orphic Argonautika*.

Neither version includes the well-known story of Médeia tricking the daughters of Pelias to cut him up and boil him. Médeia first cuts up an old goat and boils him. He is reborn from the cauldron; but when Pelias is cut up, Médeia does not revive him. This is a direct reenactment of Dionysos being cooked by the Titans.

Orpheus is on the Argo because of the magical power of his song: he is more than a *keleustes* (singer of shanties to keep the time for the rowers). According to Philóstratos' third century CE *Imagines*, Orpheus calms the stormy seas. The Argo itself is a vessel of return as it goes against time; the third century BCE *Phainómena* poem of Aratos says of the constellation Argo Navis that it follows Canis (Dog Star), travelling backwards through the sky. The Argonaut story is connected on multiple levels to Orpheus, initiation, Hyperborea, and wolves.

The legend of the Argonauts is one of the earliest known to the Greeks. It dates back possibly as far as the third or fourth millennium BCE and was known to Homer, who in the Iliad references the tale. The core of the story is extremely ancient, yet remains the same through all tellings. Aside from the Orphic and Apollónios versions, Euripides' play *Médeia* tells some of the narrative, as do Pindar's odes.

Pythian 4 tells the Argo Myth and *Olympian 3* mentions Okeanos as part of a return journey as in the *Orphic Argonautika*. In his *Historical Library*, Diódōros Sikolos gives a detailed summary of the *Argonautai* by Dionysios Skytobrachion. His was a rationalistic, humanist-liberal version.

When viewed through the two major tellings, fragments, and the artistic record, the core story is of shamanic initiation. Kheírōn the kentaur raises Iásōn on Mount Pelion. Kheírōn is initiator of young boys into the warrior-healer craft; he tends to educate the very young, whereas Orpheus is part of their final initiation. The name Kheírōn comes from *kheir* ("hand"), alluding to the skills he teaches: archery, lyre playing, mixing herbs, and healing. The kentaur taught healing to Akhilleús, Asklēpiós, and Iásōn.

Iásōn means "healer." The hero is an Apollon devotee and wolf initiate. It is very likely the earliest pre-Iliadic Iásōn was quite a different kind of figure from those of Pindar, Euripides, and Apollōnios. In Pindar's *Pythian 4*, Iásōn is described as a "very timely healer" who Paian (Apollon) himself honours.

On a fragment of a Corinthian column-crater from 575 BCE there is an Argonautic scene. A bearded Iásōn stands behind an enthroned Phineús, who is every part the Thrakian seer-king. Iásōn has both hands over Phineús' eyes while the seer shakes hands with Kástor and Polydeúkes (the Díoskouroi), indicating how Iásōn heals Phineús in early versions of the tale.

A famous late Archaic *kylix* from 500 BCE depicts a limp Iásōn emerging from the dragon's belly near the Golden Fleece as Athena watches over him. This indicates a tradition where Iásōn enters the dragon's mouth and is then disgorged – an Underworld trial. The quest of Iásōn to Kolkhís and back, and his journey into and out of the dragon's belly, are different manifestations of the descent and return.

Returning from darkness is the hardest part of the mission (be it from Kolkhís or the dragon's belly), and emergence from confinement in darkness is a crucial initiatory element of heroic transition. It is a process of personal and social benefit brought about by successful accomplishment of the hero's quest. Athena's presence on the vase is a clear indicator of the heroic nature of the task. Descent is the key to the myth and an integral part of Iásōn's healing power, which extends to the Underworld. Iásōn restores harmony between upper and lower worlds.

Iásōn as a healer fell out of favour in the Classical Greek tradition as magical healers were seen as dangerous, and their activities inappropriate for Greek heroes. His healing Zeus' ordained blindness of Phineús is a direct challenge to the order of the gods. This is perhaps why the figure of Médeia is added to later tellings of the story: the magical healing role is taken from the Greek hero and given to a foreign witch. At the heart of the oldest mythic layers is the heroic shaman-warrior of the Wolf Cult with power to heal or harm, like his patron Apollon.

Part II: The Mysteries

τα αρχαία μυστήρια

The Ancient Mysteries

The Orphic initiatory tradition degenerated over time into the Mysteries of the ancient world. These secret rites were celebrated in several places. By the time of the Romans, there were numerous "foreign" or "Eastern" mystery religions including those of Isis, Magna Mater, and Dionysos. In the Greek world, two stood out as the major Mysteries. The Eleusinian Mysteries of the mother and daughter and Samothrákian Mysteries of the Kabeiroi drew seekers from throughout the Hellenic world and beyond.

The most famous were those at Eleusís. These Underworld Mysteries were cosmological, focussed on the abduction and rape of Kórē (Persephónē) as found in the *Theogony*. These represented the first level of second sight: the shamanic sight of twilight realms and spirit animals. They were Dionysian in character.

The Samothrákian Mysteries were concentrated on the Kabeiroi as well as a trinity of protean gods called Axieros,

90

Axiokersa, and Axiokersos. These not only conveyed the cosmological level of second sight, but also the higher Apollonian metaphysical. They offered a transcendent entry to the Hyperborean realm.

The Mysteries were tantric in nature. Akin to the Vajrayana tradition, they employed multiple deities to transmit the fundamental unity of the divine presence. The initiate passed through terror and confusion before the dawning of divine light where he was admitted into the realm of light. He saw sacred visions and was "sealed," no longer subject to the suffering of the world. This tantric soul journey is described by the 4th century Eastern Roman philosopher and statesman Themístios in his work *On the Soul*, preserved by Stobaios in the 5th century.

"The soul, at the point of death has the same experience as those who are being initiated into great mysteries ... at first one wanders and wearily hurries to and fro, and journeys with suspicion through the dark as one uninitiated: then come all the terrors before the final initiation, shuddering, trembling, sweating, amazement: then one is struck with a marvellous light, one is received into pure regions and meadows, with voices and dances and the majesty of holy sounds and shapes: among these he who has fulfilled initiation wanders free, and released and bearing his crown joins in the divine communion, and consorts with pure and holy men, beholding those who live here uninitiated, an uncleansed horde, trodden under foot of him and huddled together in mud and fog, abiding in their miseries through fear of death and mistrust of the blessings there."

These Mysteries drew from an elder Orphic-Hyperborean initiatory current. This is attested in the ancient record narrating how Dionysos taught Kharops the Mysteries, who then passed them to his son Oiagros, who passed them to his son Orpheus. Orpheus is called the "revealer of *teletai*" – the *Theológos* ("singer of the gods"), teacher of a way of life. *Teletê* ("completion" or "perfection") means a religious act, mystic sacrifice, religious writing, or initiation. The plural form *teletai* ("Completions" or "Perfections") was a word used by Ancient Greeks referring to the Mysteries.

Orpheus was considered "founder" of Mystery religions and the initiatic tradition. In the Grove of the Muses at Thespia, a statue of the goddess "Mystery" stood next to Orpheus. According to Plato in his *Republic* and Aristophanes in his *Frogs*, Orpheus revealed to men the *teletai*. Plato says that initiates into the mysteries are "true philosophers" in his *Phaido* while both Diódōros and Pausanias connect the Orphic writings to the Mysteries, but note it as a "literary tradition" – an ancient current, not a formal religion.

The Hyperborean Mystery tradition came into Europe via Thraki. It then embedded itself into the fertile spiritual environment of Greece. The Platonists and Chaldeans then preserved it through Theurgy into the latter part of antiquity. Theurgists explicitly based their work on the Mysteries. They conducted their rituals at night in wild areas outdoors, alone or in small groups. Iámblikhos connects the Mysteries to Theurgy in his work *On the Mysteries*.

The *Chaldean Oracles* that have come down through antiquity in fragment form were highly praised by the Neoplatonists Iámblikhos and Proklos. These were not from Chaldea (Babylon), but written by Julian the Chaldean and his son Julian the Theurge. The word "Chaldean" was used to denote a "mystic" or "magician" in the Roman world, and Chaldean Theurgy was a direct descendent of the ancient Mystery tradition.

"A certain knowledge of the way of things engendered within us by superior beings, revealed by autoptic manifestations and the guidance of the gods who disclose the order of the universe to souls, guide our journey to the Intelligible, and kindle the fires that lead upward." (*Chaldean Oracles* fragment 189 from Proklos, *Alkibiádēs* 87)

Ἐλευσίς

Eleusís

The Mysteries at Eleusís were the most famous in the ancient world. The Eleusinian Mysteries initiated seekers for two millennia, from the Bronze Age until the closure of the Mysteries by order of Theodosios I in 392 CE. Originally open only to the members of the Eleusinian elite, then over time to Athenians, then speakers of Greek, initiates could eventually be found across the Mediterranean.

The secret of what was revealed at the Mysteries has remained undisclosed. The likely reason these secrets remained with the initiates is that the initiation was not expressible in words. The revelation was a non-logical set of images and myths that defied communication to those who had not experienced them.

What can be ascertained is that the mythos was in line with that told in the 7th century BCE *Homeric Hymn to Dēmétēr*. The synopsis is:

While picking flowers with her companions including Artemis, Persephónē-Kórē (daughter of Dēmḗtēr) is abducted by Hā́idēs, Lord of the Underworld. Hekátē hears her cries and Helios sees the abduction. She is taken to his shadowy realm where she is made his bride. Dēmḗtēr searches for her, carrying torches to light her way for nine days. On the dawn of the tenth day, Hekátē comes to her and says she heard something. The pair then go to Helios who tells them that Zeus, father of Persephónē, allowed Hā́idēs to take the girl as his bride.

Dēmḗtēr withdraws from the assembly of the gods and roams the earth in grief. She eventually arrives at Eleusís where she is seen as an old woman by the daughters of king Keleós. They question her, and Dēmḗtēr says she is from Krete and that she was abducted by pirates but escaped. She tells them she is a nursemaid, and the princesses bring her to their mother Métaneira who has an infant son, Demophöon. The goddess sits in grief until a servant, Iámbe ("banter"), jests and makes her laugh. Offered wine, the goddess declines and asks for a *kykeôn* made of barley and mint leaves.

Dēmḗtēr becomes the nurse of Demophöon, who she anoints with ambrosia and places in the fire each night to make him immortal. One night, Métaneira witnesses this and cries out. Angered, the goddess reveals her true form and says she would have made the boy immortal, but now he will share the same lot as other mortals. She then demands they build her a temple and says that she will give them rites with which to propitiate her.

The temple is built and Dēmḗtēr occupies it. In her grief, she does not let the seed sprout for a year, bringing a terrible famine to the world. Zeus sends Îris (messenger of the gods) to fetch her, but Dēmḗtēr refuses until she sees her daughter. Zeus then sends Hermês to the Underworld to fetch Persephónē; Haîdēs allows this, but feeds her a pomegranate seed. Persephónē then travels back to the earth on Haîdēs' golden chariot.

Mother and daughter are reunited, but Dēmḗtēr tells Persephónē if she tasted food in the Underworld she will have to spend a third of every year with Haîdēs. Hekátē becomes Persephónē's chief attendant, and Zeus promises honours for Dēmḗtēr and Persephónē. He also reiterates the girl must spend one third of the year in the Underworld, with the rest among the Olympians. Dēmḗtēr returns life to earth, allowing barley to grow. She then teaches the Mystery rites to the elites of Eleusís.

The hymn then ends with an admonition that the rites *"are not to be transgressed, nor pried into, nor divulged. For great awe of the gods stops the voice. Blessed is the mortal on earth who has seen these rites, but the uninitiate who has no share in them never has the same lot once dead in the dreary darkness."*

This mythic narrative was played out to some degree by the initiates in the Telesterion (inner sanctuary). The *hierophantēs* showed an object – some believe to be an ear of barley – as a revelation signifying rebirth after death. This object was kept along with other sacred items in the Anaktoron ("palace"): the sanctum sanctorum within the Telesterion.

Those initiated left with a profound sense of happiness and satisfaction with life, knowing they would have a better lot in the afterlife. Wandering through dark in terror and confusion, an initiate was suddenly struck by marvellous light and received into pure regions. He was free from fear of death.

It was said in the ancient world that Orpheus made his presence felt at the Eleusinian Mysteries, despite not being a specific part of them. The secrets of Hāidēs were considered to be in Orpheus' possession. He could tell his followers what awaited them.

The cult of Dēmétēr in Eleusís began in the 15th century BCE. The Eleusinian Mysteries were said to be of Thrakian or Thessalian origin. The *líknon*, a winnowing fan used ritually at Eleusís, was held over the head of the initiate. This conveys the importance of grain in the Mysteries, perhaps signifying the separation of body and soul as grain from chaff, since Dēmétēr and Kórē represent a dual chthonic fertility goddess. This likely has a Thrakian origin.

When the hero Odysseus is in the North to perform rites to Poseidon to gain the god's forgiveness, he is told to stop at the place his oar is mistaken for a winnowing fan. This is in Thraki, from whence Orpheus transmitted the mysteries. It was also stated in the ancient mythic record that Eúmolpos ("good singer") of Thraki fought alongside the Eleusinians against the Athenians of Erekhtheús.

The Eleusinians lost the battle, but retained the right to perform the Mysteries. Eúmolpos was said to be the "first celebrant of the Mysteries;" he was a mythical king considered to be a warrior-priest of either Dēmétēr or Dionysos. It is also stated that Eleusís was named after the legendary Eleusís son of Ogygos ("the Primaeval One"), a mythical ruler of Boiōtía in the North of Greece.

Originally the Mysteries were only open to the *aristoi* ("nobles") of Eleusís. Later, only murderers and non-Greeks were excluded. Murder is an impure act and ritual purity was a prerequisite. Initiates were called *ói ósioi* ("the Pure"), as were Orphic initiates. A ram's pelt – the "fleece of Zeus" or "purifying fleece" was used to purify those tainted with blood. This has the same function as the Golden Fleece of the Argonaut myth. The whole Eleusinian festival was one of purification, which links it also to Apollon, as he is the purifying god.

In Proklos' *Orphic Fragments* we learn that Kórē first bore children to Apollon: "*[Dēmétēr speaks to Kórē] But going up to the fruitful bed of Apollon, thou shalt bear splendid children with countenances of flaming fire*" and "*[Kórē bears] nine daughters, grey eyed, makers of flowers.*" (*Fragments* 194 and 197)

Another figure associated with the Mysteries was Iakkhos. The procession from Athens to Eleusís was led by bearers of a statue of this god. His only function was to lead the soon-to-be-initiated to the site. Iakkhos was son of Zeus Khthónios ("Zeus of the Underworld," i.e. Hā́idēs) and Persephónē. Iakkhos was associated with Dionysos, which ties in with Dionysos' birth in the *Orphic Theogony*.

Iakkhos is Dionysos as the torchbearer at Eleusís, and according to Lucanus "fire is a Dionysian weapon." Rites to Iakkhos were performed to negate the ill effects of the Dog Star and bring bountiful harvest. Thus, Iakkhos was the light-bringing star of the nocturnal mysteries.

Hā́idēs was also a fertility god: Ploutōn ("Wealth"). At Eleusís, the Ploutonion was the first cave temple at the beginning of the sacred way into the sanctuary. Ploutonia were considered direct inlets to the Underworld. Hā́idēs is the "invisible" or "invisible-making" in contrast to Helios the "visible" or "visible-making." Thus, the initiates first had to enter the invisible realm of the dead before entering the sanctuary.

In Greek religion, *psychopompeia* were clefts in the rock through which souls pass like the wind. This wind-soul aspect is intrinsically connected to the wolf and the Wolf Cult. Hermês was the psychopomp ("leader of the dead") par excellence, but Dionysos as "master of the souls" of the dead held a similar function at Eleusís under the title of Iakkhos.

At the heart of the Eleusinian Mysteries were Dēmḗtēr and Kórē. In the myth and in imagery at Eleusís, the goddesses Artemis and Hekátē were also present. Dēmḗtēr the mother and

Kórē the maiden preside over grain, poppies, and trees, the first two of which featured heavily in the rites. In the myth, Artemis, the violent virgin huntress, is with Kórē-Persephónē prior to her abduction.

Hekátē, the vengeful dark mother, appears alongside Dēmétēr when she is raging in grief. Orpheus calls Artemis Hekátē in the *Orphic Argonautika*, conflating the pair of torchbearers of the Eleusinian imagery. Hekátē is specifically Queen of Souls who are eastbound to the upper world. Underworld Hermês is her masculine counterpart and both these gods also featured at Samothráki.

While fertility was part of the ritual at Eleusís, the true ripening was of the initiates, with grain representing renewal of life. These four goddesses are really all aspects of the same Queen of the Underworld. Gaîa or Gê ("Earth") is the original Underworld goddess with mantic abilities. At some point in deep antiquity, this primordial goddess gave way to several later manifestations of the Goddess.

These include Dēmétēr and Kórē. Like Gaîa, both are associated with souls and crops (Dēmétēr at Eleusís is Earth, and Kórē is corn grain). Both are aspects of the Underworld Queen and particularly associated with the moon. The moon was seen as a force that ripened crops, which may be one reason why the rites of "ripening" were held at night. The Mysteries being held at night also points to an Orphic origin, implying the goddess Nyx ("Night") is mother of gods and Light is born of Darkness.

The grain aspect of the Mysteries took precedence over time with the mythic figure of Triptólemos ("Tripartite Warrior") assuming a mission of dispersing grain throughout the world. In this function he came to represent the new plant. This was not his original function however. The "Tripartite Warrior" is possibly connected to the ancient Proto-Indo-European figure of Trito, the first warrior and dragon-slayer. His other name is Buzyges ("Bull-hitcher"), connecting him to the Orphic Dionysos myth and slaying of the god in bull form.

Another grain aspect that may have lost meaning over time is the *kykeôn*. This barley drink was imbibed by initiates after fasting to induce visions. The contents of the *kykeôn* have been disputed since antiquity, but two candidates seem likely considering the imagery invoked at Eleusís.

Both barley and poppies are at the forefront, and these two plants still grow abundantly among the ruins to this day. *Opion* (poppy juice) was used to induce ritual death in Ancient Greece, and the ergot grain rust of barley is a source of lysergic acid diethylamide (LSD). The ergot of barley was specifically associated with Apollon Lykeios ("Apollon the Wolf God").

The Athenian Lykomidai family, who took their name from their ancestor Lykomédēs ("wolf counsel"), held the office of *Dadoûkhos* ("torchbearer") at the Eleusinian Mysteries. They also held their own private Mystery rites at Phlya near Athens, during which they sung the songs of Orpheus.

Perhaps under layers of accumulated imagery and ritual lies a more ancient Mystery Cult at the heart of the Eleusinian Mysteries – one involving ritual death and rebirth of a warrior elite. Perhaps these Mystery rites degenerated over time from a more "Orphic" version.

The Mysteries at Eleusís had no carryover into daily life like in the Orphic religion. To be assured of the protection of the great goddesses and a blessed life after death, one had merely to perform the ritual, see the sights, and say the words. The original Orphic initiation was not just sights and sounds, but had a heavily visionary aspect. Initiates of the Eleusinian Mysteries went to Elysion after death, but needed to perform no further acts after initiation nor lead a moral life.

This initiation-for-all, salvationary religion was far removed from its original state. The irony of this did not escape ancient thinkers (despite their awe of the gods), leading the great cynic philosopher Diogenes of Sinope to say, "Because he has been initiated at Eleusís, Pataikon the thief will have a better fate after his death than Agesilaos and Epimeinondas."

The Eleusinian Mysteries give some clues as to the original Hyperborean initiation, but more can be found by examining the more ancient secret rites at Samothráki in the North.

Σαμοθράκη

Samothráki

Samothráki is a portal to the Spiritual North. Since deepest antiquity, the island lying a few miles off the coast of Thraki in Northern Greece has been sacred. It has a mountain that dramatically juts out of the sea, invoking the Cosmic Mountain of Hyperborea: a sacred peak surrounded by water. The mountain Fengári ("Moon") occupies the centre of Samothráki, which can be translated as the "Heights of Thraki."

Filled with the magnetic green rocks permeating the island, the Sanctuary of the Great Gods is aligned Northward. The mountain of Fengári is to the south of the sanctuary, which centres around a smooth green sacred rock resembling a mountain in shape. The alignment is not to our current North, but is directed towards the star Thuban in the constellation Draco. At the time the megaliths were raised in Europe – from the fourth to the second millennia BCE – the polestar was in Draco, which was a much bigger constellation encompassing both bears.

The sacred porphyritic lodestone boulder north of the Hieron means the sanctuary always points North to Hyperborea, even when the polestar changes. This magnetism was a critical part of the mysteries. All around the sanctuary are magnetic rocks, while the sign of initiates was a magnetic ring and purple fillet. Magnetism and initiation are both invisible, but their effects can nonetheless be felt.

This magnetic sanctuary was dedicated to the Megáloi Theoí ("Great Gods") or Kábeiroi, a trio or pair of chthonic deities. It was taboo to use their true names, but the three names used on Samothráki were Axieros (male deity), Axiokersa (female deity), and Axiokersos (male deity). These names are pre-Greek, as was the language used in the Mystery rites. As with most magical ritual, words of invocation cannot be changed even if the language is no longer understood – which into the Roman era was the case with the Samothrákian Mysteries.

While these three were principal deities on the island, and the mysteries utilised various gods, the ancient record speaks specifically of twin gods. The "sacred light of the two *Kabeiroi*," or "twin lights of the Kabeiroi," or "doubly sacred light of Kabeiros in Samothráki" were all terms used to describe the power of the Mysteries. The Roman writer Varro describes a pair of ithyphallic statues in both the harbour of Samothráki and at the sanctuary. These he equated to Kástor and Polydeúkes, the Díoskouroi ("Zeus' boys"), patrons of seafaring travellers. Ptolemy considered the sacred twins to be Apollon and Herakles.

While there are merits in both of these, they are not the likely candidates since Kástor and Polydeúkes were both Argonauts who were initiated into the Mysteries, and Apollon and Herakles are simply sons of Zeus. The three names of the gods (Axieros, Axiokersa, Axiokersos) were not Greek. These names were likely transmitted from the Phrygians via Thraki. The original inhabitants of the island were Pelasgoí (Pelasgians), Indo-Europeans who came from Western Asia and settled on Samothráki. The name was given by the Greeks to the people they encountered as they swept into Greece. The name Pelasgoí likely derives from *pélas* ("near" – i.e. neighbour). According to Herodotos, they were highly religious and did not mention their gods by name, which corresponds to the nameless gods of Samothráki.

The female deity Axiokersa is likely the Mountain Mother, called Kybele by the Phrygians. This Mountain Goddess has many names: Rhea, Kybele, Agdystis, and so on. She is almost always associated with the lion (like Durga in India), and is sometimes the Mistress of Animals, a role also filled by Artemis. On Samothraki she could likewise be called Leukothea ("White Goddess"). She is mother of the gods, especially in the Thrakian tradition of Sabazios, the sky god horse rider associated with both Zeus and Dionysos.

The Greek goddess Rhea is the Mountain Mother who bore Zeus to Kronos, then transformed into Dēmétēr. As Dēmétēr she bore Persephónē to Zeus, who in turn bore Dionysos to Zeus.

Sabazios is Zagreus: the first Dionysos, son of Zeus and Persephónē, torn apart and cooked by Titans. Zeus saves his heart and impregnates Semelē (the Thrako-Phyrigian name for the earth goddess), siring a second Dionysos: Dionysos Khthónios, who was born a third time from Zeus' thigh. In his mythos, Sabazios was cut apart but his ithyphallic genitals were recovered by the Kabeiroi of Samothráki and kept upright at the heart of the mysteries.

Phrygians are found referenced throughout the mythic and historical record. They lie at the roots of both the Northern Sabazios tradition and Southern Zagreus tradition. Sabazios came into the Greek religion from the Phrygians via the Thrakians; Zagreus was transmitted from the Phrygians via the Kretans. He is one god, thrice-born, and two-natured.

The two male gods in the trio are referred to as "Celestial Twins," "Mighty Lords," and "Masters of Samothráki." According to the *Orphic Hymn to the Kouretes*, these two warrior deities *"dwell in the sacred land of Samothráki."*

The Mountain Mother is traditionally accompanied by a retinue of Kouretes or Korybantes in the Phrygian tradition. These Kouretes were the "first to develop sacred rites for humans." Axieros and Axiokersos are therefore likely to be Kouretes, the armed warrior ecstatics who attended Zeus when he was an infant. The "k" sound (i.e. "ak"/"ax" in Proto-Indo-European) denotes the "sharpness" of weapons; in Greek *akḗ* means "point."

The islands of Imbros, Lemnos, and some cities of the Troad of Asia Minor (such as Pergamon and Miletos) also had sanctuaries of the Kabeiroi. Investigation into the nature of their cults yields information that helps to reveal more about Samothrákian worship. The ancient consensus was that there were two male Kabeiroi and an associated female deity. This makes the Kabeiroi a pair of gods with a female who is always with them.

On Samothráki, according to Hesiod *Fragment 177*, Ēléktrā gave birth to Dárdanos and Ēetíōn. The historian Mnaséas relates that Dárdanos arrived on Samothráki with his sister Harmonía and brother Iasíōn. Diódōros Sikolos states that Iasíōn founded the Mysteries of Samothráki, married Cybele, and fathered Korybas.

The names of the triad are interchangeable, but not the composition. The gods' names changed continually from Pelasgian to Greek to Roman, but the language of the mysteries was ancient and incomprehensible to Greeks and Romans. The nameless Megáloi Theoí, protean gods, remained at the heart of the mysteries.

Byzantine grammarian Stéphanos Byzántios says that *"Imbros is sacred to the Kabeiroi and Hermes, whom the Karians call Imbrasos."* It is clear the Imbrians and Samothrákians worshipped the same gods. The Kabeiroi mysteries of Lemnos were also related to Samothrákian. The Kabeiroi there had an older male and a younger one and were named Héphaistos and Kamillos, who is likely Hermês. Héphaistos worship is particular to Lemnos, so his inclusion in the triad is likely isolated to the island.

At Pergamon the *Kabeirion* was particularly associated with the *gymnasion* and initiation of the *ephēboi*. The sacrifice of a ram was prominent, as it was on Samothráki. There is a close connection between the initiation of the *ephēboi* and Mystery rites of the Kabeiroi. Miletos also had a sanctuary of the Kabeiroi situated outside the main city (in Assessos), as was the case at Samothráki, Imbros, Lemnos, and Thebes.

The myth associated with the rites at Miletos come to us from the Roman historian Nikolāos Damaskēnos. He says the sons of the murdered king Lāodámās had taken refuge in Assessos. The besieged princes received help from two young men from Phrygia. The two youths, Tottes and Onnes, brought a chest with the *hiéra* ("holy objects") of the Kabeiroi. After a sacrifice, the sons of Lāodámās and their army confronted their foes with the chest at the head of their phalanx, secured victory, and reasserted their rights to the throne. These *hiéra* became part of the mysteries at Miletos.

These two Phrygian youths are clearly manifestations of the divine twins. That they are described as non-Greek suggests a "non-Greek" appearance like the ithyphallic statues of Samothráki. The great goddess of Assessos was Athena, who was widely worshipped in neighbouring Karia and Ionia. Votive evidence found throughout the region infers a more ancient divinity lies behind Athena. Here we see a goddess with two male youths; in the Milesian variant of the cult there was a close connection between youths, war, and the Kabeiroi, suggesting a coming-of-age ritual in the background of the myth.

In Thebes, worship of the Kabeiroi was denoted by a prominence of male youths, also suggesting an ephebic initiation. Pais ("boy"), Kabeiros, and Mḗtēr ("mother") were the trio of deities at Thebes, where there was also a grove of Dēmḗtēr and Kórē. This Theban worship may have been influenced by Eleusís. There is also a strong Dionysian imagery about Kabeiros and Pais, both of whom are often crowned with ivy. Pais is normally depicted pouring wine for Kabeiros.

The Kabeiroi are often referred to as "Titans" in the ancient accounts, and the ecstatic dancing that formed part of their mysteries positively connects the Kabeiroi to the Kouretes or Korybantes. Drinking was also part of the final stage of initiation at almost all of their mystery centres. Scholars often draw the conclusion of an interface between Greek and Anatolian (Luwian/Hittite) Indo-European initiatic expressions. This is likely, but only possible as the two strands connect to the deeper Hyperborean root.

The Phrygian Korybantes were the first men seen by the sun god when they shot up like trees in the Anatolian tradition. The Samothrákian Korybantes were said by the mythographer Pherekydes of Syros to be sons of Apollon and Rhêtia (an Oreiad nymph of Mount Saon on Samothráki). The Korybantes were not the Kabeiroi, but ecstatic dancers of the Mysteries numbering either seven or nine. Rhêtia was likely the goddess who presided over reciting to new initiates the lore of the Mysteries.

Here the Apollonian connection is established and the Korybantes explicitly named in the ritual process. Korybantic rites were ecstatic, delivering divine madness to participants. Unlike the Mainadic rites of Dionysian worship, according to Plato these Korybantic rites were originally open only to aristocratic men. They involved a *krater* ("wine cup") ritual which naturally precluded women, as wine drinking was often forbidden to them.

The verb *korybantiaô* ("to be mad") equates the Korybantes as male counterparts to the Mainades. These were Apollonian male ecstatics mirroring Dionysian female ecstatics. Korybantic rites were later opened to women who came to dominate them.

Three deities were particularly worshipped at Samothráki. However, many gods and deified hero figures were associated with the sanctuary and Megáloi Theoí. Dionysos, Orpheus, Haḯdēs, Persephónē, Hekátē, Dēmétēr, the Korybantes, Kadmillos (an ithyphallic god associated with Hermês), the Díoskouroi, and Kadmos and Harmonía (also called Kadmillos and Ēléktrā – "amber") were all present in some form or other.

The last two were sometimes a pairing for the *Hieròs Gámos* ("sacred marriage") featured in the mystery rites. Another

Samothrakian *heiros logos* ("sacred story") is the rape of Dēmétēr by Iasíōn as the *Hieròs Gámos*. All of these are tied together by the goddess Persephónē, who connects with all of them.

In his work *The Deities of Samothrace*, German philosopher Friedrich Schelling saw an ascending series of deities, much as those found in theurgy. At the lowest end was Dēmétēr, who to Schelling represented hunger or seeking; next was Persephónē, essence or fundamental origin of the visible world. Then came Dionysos, Lord of the Spirit World, followed finally by Kadmillos-Hermês who was above nature and Spirit World: a mediator between them and transcendence. This "Kabeiroi doctrine" of Schelling was a system of ascent from the subordinate nature deities up to a transcendent god. In essence, Kabeiroi were theurgic and brought higher gods into realisation; for the initiate became a *kabir*, or link in the magical chain.

While Schelling's work is not perfect, it encapsulates the spirit of the initiatic experience. It demonstrates a tantric climb to transcendence through the god archetypes. From the Earth Mother Dēmétēr, the initiate next encounters Persephónē (Queen of the Underworld), who returns him to nature; this represents death and rebirth and the goddess is aided in this by Hekátē, Queen of Spirits. Next encountered is Persephónē's son by Zeus, Dionysos, whose epithet is Eleutherios ("he who makes free"). He mediates between natural and spiritual worlds, while Hermês (messenger of the gods) gives the seeker a direct esoteric initiation – a revelation of the divine.

While this may not have been the genuine experience at Samothráki, ancient paganism was externally polytheistic, but esoterically these deities were all expressions of the Absolute. The mysteries revealed the initiate's own transcendent nature: the Self that surpasses time. The nameless protean Megáloi Theoí remained on the inner terrain, visible only to the inner eye of inspiration. On the "far side" of revelation is the divine. This is the advantage of initiatory tantric polytheism over so-called monotheism (in reality monolatrism), serving only to block the human experience of the divine through nature.

This initiatic experience is revealed somewhat through the Platonic tradition which had a long history of connection to the Mysteries, beginning with Plato himself. Philosophy is the spiritual process to gain direct knowledge of the divine and realise Truth for oneself. Platonic mysticism recognises multiple deities and the fundamental unity of a divine presence, akin somewhat to Vajrayana Buddhism.

What we know of the actual initiations at Samothraki is limited. They danced at some point and upon completion had a symposium-style feast replete with plentiful wine. They received an iron magnetic ring and a purple fillet upon initiation.

The scholiast on Apollṓnios Rhódios states: *"They say Odysseus, being an initiate and using Leukothea's veil in place of a fillet, was saved from the storm at sea by placing the veil below his abdomen. For the initiates bind fillets below their abdomens."* We also know initiates likely searched for Harmonía (Persephónē) at the first stage of initiation, possibly as an Underworld search for the maiden like at Eleusís. This is also reflected in the myth of Orpheus entering the underworld to retrieve his bride.

We hear from the Roman polymath Varro that the Herm (ithyphallic Hermês statue) was taken by the Athenians from the Pelasgians of Samothráki. He says that Hermês, son of Ouranos and Hemera was aroused by the sight of Persephónē and that this was a *heiros logos* of the Samothrakian mysteries. Kallimakhos calls this ithyphallic god Kasmillos. There is thus a sacred marriage between Kasmillos and Harmonía.

The Goddess

On Samothráki a goddess forms part of the Kabeiric trinity. This goddess has had many names through history. The gods generally have many names, but behind these is their divine nature. Gods manifest divinity. They are dynamic and unfixed. The barrier between gods and men is permeable as we share a continuum with the gods and nature.

The goddess of Samothráki is an earth mother. She has various aspects but is often identified with Hekátē, the Queen of Spirits. A cave of Hekátē is located at Zerynthos on other side of Samothráki from the sanctuary. Hekátē is often depicted as three bodied, a crossroads goddess. She is associated with the Underworld and night.

Hekátē is leader of the pack of dogs and bearer of light in darkness. She is an ancient Titan honoured by Zeus after he takes power. Even the King of the Gods understands she is a powerful ally and dangerous enemy. She is a manifestation of Nyx (Night) and in her fearful aspect is called Brimo. She is also called Bendis, Persephónē, Dēmétēr, Kybele, Rhea, and Artemis. These are all different aspects and names of an underlying force.

On Samothráki certain aspects of Hekátē are prominent, but particularly her psychopomp facet. In the mythos, Hekátē took Dēmétēr to the Underworld to search for Persephónē-Kórē. After the *Titanomakhia,* new gods existed in continuity with the old, but had dominion over them. When the Zeus *Kosmos* was created, she was the only Titan to be given authority in the new order, having dominion over the Sky, Earth, and Underworld. Like her male counterpart Hermês, she can pass between realms. She is unique among ancient deities in that she is associated with both the Underworld and *Kosmos.*

Hekátē is a guide of souls, but identified specifically with the soul of the *Kosmos* in total, and ensoulment of humans upon birth. She is closely involved in human destiny and their afterlife. She is in triplicate form in statuary and carries two torches, aligning with the concept of "twin lights of the Kabeiroi." Hekátē is Sophia, divine revealer in the Chaldean Oracles and Platonism. Associated with *inyx* wheels (wheels of destiny), Hekátē the Cosmic Soul is spirit guide at Samothráki.

Identified with the dog, Hekátē is also goddess of the pack. Dog and wolf are interchangeable in many respects through mythology. In her aspect as Artemis, she leads the Wild Hunt.

In the Orphic tradition Artemis is called Hekátē. The *Second Idyll* of Theokritos has Simaitha the Magician cursing: *"O Artemis, Hast power hells' adamant to shatter down every stubborn thing. Hark! Thestylis, Hekátē's hounds are baying up the town, the goddess at the crossroads."*

Hekátē's hounds are the dead and ritually dead: Wolf Warriors. Thus the goddess is connected to the initiatic Wolf Cult. The Wolf Warrior band has since deep antiquity been under the aegis of a female deity with many names and aspects.

On Samothráki, Hekátē is sometimes called Ēléktrā. She is also known as Strategis. She protects the band during its voyages, skirmishes, adventures, incursions, and plundering.

Twins

A pair of statues, ithyphallic twins, guarded the sanctuary at Samothráki. The twins motif was particularly heightened on the island with the Díoskouroi and Gemini constellation invoked by both ancient and modern scholarship. These divine twins are the two males of the Kabeiric trinity: Axieros and Axiokersos. They are potent warriors encapsulating pure male virility and energy.

115

The Korybantes are warriors in service to the great goddess of the mountains, and these Kabeiroi are also closely connected with the mountain mother. Their erections stand in relation to the female principle. They represent the heavenly masculine complementing the earthly feminine. The erect phallus can also represent ecstasy induced by the war dance of the Korybantes.

If we examine the sacred tale of Samothráki once again, we see that only one ithyphallic male is mentioned: Kadmillos, or Hermês. Hermês is the god who conjures luminous light out of the dark abyss – a spellbinder of oaths with the power to bind and release: "the one who holds down." The *Etymologicum Magnum* (374.23) says of Hermês: *"The Father called him the Clever One because he excelled all the blessed gods and mortal men in gainful crafts and stealthy skills."*

The gods do not conform to rational constructs and bourgeois moral codes, but manifest frighteningly transcendent power. Thus he who is "initiated into the mysteries of Hermês" understands the god has another function in his ithyphallic aspect: he symbolises the generation of the Spirit. As in the Indian tradition, uterine blood carries Spirit, energy, and soul; the erect penis incarnates spirit unto flesh through seminal fluid. Therefore, male and female genitals symbolise, reveal, and embody the sacred.

Early Christian church father Hippólytos of Rome states in his *Refutation of All Heresies* (5.8.9): *"Two statues of naked men in the Anaktoron of the Samothrákians with both hands stretched up*

116

towards heaven and the pudenda turned up, just like the statue of
Hermês at Kyllene. The aforesaid statues are images of the primal man
and of the regenerated, spiritual man who is in every respect
consubstantial with that man."

From this passage we gain some insight into the nature of the twins at Samothráki. They symbolise the celestial and chthonic twins like the Díoskouroi, where one is of earth and the other heaven. The earthly man below has a counterpart in the man of light above. The twins relate to initiates in that they can be regenerated into their original celestial nature; there are twin realms and the Spirit has a higher origin.

Just as the Orphic plate instructs, *"I am a child of Earth and starry Heaven; but my race is of Heaven (alone),"* the primal archaic symbolism of the twins provide a means of realising our own higher dimensions – of achieving transcendence that takes us beyond to the abode of the Race of Light. The magnetic doubleness of Samothráki begins to come into clarity once we grasp the twins' meaning. The magnetic ring of Samothráki mirrors the alignment of the sanctuary to the North; in the North are the Gemini and Draco constellations, both of which are twins. The serpent represents the manifestation of the divine – the dual serpent is thus doubly potent in meaning.

Standing in the parallel worlds of men and gods, the seeker is initiated at Samothráki into the Mysteries of the North, of the celestial and earthly twins. He sees that each of us on earth has a celestial twin, or as Neoplatonist Plōtînos calls him in his

Enneads: *"our allowed guardian spirit."* The celestial twin is the "spiritual man" who has realised his identity with his primordial Spirit prior to this Fallen Age. Arthur Versluis states in his *Entering the Mysteries, "Into this fleeting horizontally temporal human life can be introduced the lightning bolt of the vertical divine, the flash in the darkness of illumination."* It is thus that the initiate at Samothráki came to know his twin nature.

Water

A purple strip of cloth was worn around the waist of initiates while at sea. In the Iliad, Poseidon sits on Samothráki to watch the Trojan war. The god was tied to the island in the Archaic period. Poseidon was a Pelasgian god of the early Indo-European tradition; he was the "Earth Shaker" and his name can translate to "Lord of the Earth." His domain is the sea and he created the horse on Mount Pelion in Thessaly, the mountain home of the kentaur Kheírōn. The god also has a wind aspect as on both horse and ship man is conveyed "by the wind." His trident represents the World Axis and three realms: Underworld, Ocean, and World Above. This makes the water, land, and air all realms of Poseidon.

Poseidon came to be connected with Samothráki through association to Nereus, god of the Aegean Sea, which the Samothrákian sanctuary overlooks. Nereus is also called Proteus ("First"), as he is a primaeval god associated with both Samothráki and Lemnos. In ancient thought, the three *Kabeiroi* were children of Kabeiro, a daughter of Proteus. In the Odyssey, Menelaos tells how he captures Proteus and guarantees his entry in the Elysian Fields.

This is an important clue as to the nature of Proteus and what he conveys. Proteus is primordial, divine nature capable of shapeshifting through forms. His daughter Thetis sheltered Dionysos under the sea for a time. Thetis changes form through a series of transformations to try and escape Peleus, father of Akhilleús. Dionysos, who is the "Liberator" also changes form.

In the Orphic myth Dionysos-Zagreus shifts form while fighting the Titans. He is also protean, having human form, but able to transform effortlessly between forms and realms. Proteus/Nereus, his daughter Thetis, and Dionysos are fluid.

Water has many forms. It can be both gentle and violent; it can be waves, sea foam, mist, clouds, fog, rain, ice, snow, and steam. Regardless of what form it takes, it is still water. Metaphysically, water represents the underlying unity of forms. It offers the understanding that while we are in our current form, that is not our absolute or true form: we have a higher Self.

Homer's Wine Dark Sea is, in this meaning, a metaphor for human life. These obscure, uncertain waters must be navigated in order to reach the far shore of understanding. Nereus or Proteus represents the divine guidance that can return us home to a Hyperborean state.

Water also carries the power of purification. Lustral waters wash away accumulated dirt of manifestation, returning one to a pristine unity of Being as in the beginning. Water cleanses man, revealing the purity of his timeless existence. It is this purifying aspect that also connects the mysteries to Apollon. As the purifying god, Apollon was present.

The island goddess was often called Ēléktrā, a solar name implying amber, which is sacred to Apollon. The ancient name for Samothráki was Melité, connoting honey and bees, both linked to Apollon – as are music and dance, which were central to the sacred rites. Most importantly in relation to water, Apollon is connected to the sea through the dolphin (whence the name Delphoi). The dolphin joyfully cuts though the waves, transcending Self and journeying between worlds, fusing human and divine through the ecstatic state.

Hieròs Gámos

The *Hieròs Gámos* ("Holy Union" or "Sacred Marriage") was one of the final initiatic stages of the Samothrákian Mysteries. The *Hieròs Gámos* is often between Zeus and Hera in the exoteric Greek tradition, but on Samothráki is played out by different deities. This Holy Union is much like that of gods and goddesses in the Tantric tradition of the East. In the Age of Iron we must recognise ourselves in our divinities, so that they may see us and we may reach towards them – and then beyond.

Gods and goddesses have both positive and negative qualities. Hera, for example, is capable of being a devoted wife and mother, giving protection to those she loves, but is also angry and spiteful. Hekátē is frightful and dark, but a healer. Dionysos is terror inducing, but a liberator. Like wrathful Tantric gods they are vehicles. We must recognise their divinity and use them to transform our darkness; we must transmute it to liberate ourselves.

The Mysteries used nightmarish images, sexuality, food, wine, dance, and music, just as in the Tantric paths of India and beyond to the East. These were all transformed by the religious nature of the Mysteries. The *Hieròs Gámos* represents transmutation of the negative. The Samothrákian Mysteries were held to be morally upright, making an initiate a more honourable person. This was achieved through transmutation, not renunciation.

On Samothráki Harmonía is a form of Persephónē. She is rescued by Kadmos (Kadmillos-Hermês) resulting in their reunion and sexual pairing, symbolised by ithyphallic imagery. The ithyphallic male represents an unapologetic embrace of life. It is return to the primordial state without shame.

Vitality and beauty are part of the sacred path. This primordiality is why the Mysteries were associated with elder gods (the Titans) by ancient writers. Kronos, king of the Titans, rules over the Isles of the Blessed, which exists in a perpetual Golden Age.

The *Hieròs Gámos* is the positive and negative re-emergence of primordial humanity beyond time. It is a revelation of timelessness, light, and the magnetic power of life manifested at a sacred site through ritual. This is both external and internal: a divine wedding between different aspects of the Self, as well as man and gods. It is the restoration of primal unity.

After ritual death an initiate experiences the "two lights." This is a two-in-one unity of timeless eternity in the Isles of the Blessed. The marriage symbolises reuniting the two parts of the Self: the Twins.

Light

The climax of the Mysteries was observing a great light – the revelation of "light in the dark." A first century BCE inscription reads, *"As an initiate, great hearted, he saw the doubly sacred light of Kabeiros in Samothráki."*

The initiate goes to an illuminated state in death: the *khorós eusébion* or "region of the reverent." In his *Phaidros*, Plato tells how initiates beheld a pure, shining light. This was the Anthrôpos or "Man of Light." This concept was absorbed into Gnosticism and also the Qabbālā as Adam Kadmon. Both of these esoteric traditions took liberally from Platonism and the Mysteries.

Primordial man is an Unconditioned Being. The man living in time must acknowledge the celestial timeless Absolute Twin above temporality. The conditioned human and unconditioned man form a celestial double – the ultimate Self. This was the message of Empedokles' *Purifications*, where states of being flow into each other and man is capable of rebirth and reincarnation into a god state.

It is this figure of the Anthrôpos that Arthur Versluis sees in Orpheus in his *Enter the Mysteries*: *"The hero, healer, and priest, the prophet and seer, the magus or theurge and poet musician all in one represents the most archaic figure whom Orpheus also symbolises. The archaic hierophant is the primordial dweller on the island, the first one, but the one who belongs to no time, indeed, is beyond time."*

What is timeless is always present; the mysteries are still accessible. Orpheus is still an initiator and can be found where he has always been: within the seeker himself. The inquirer is able to use the telestic art of the Theurge to become a vehicle for the gods. Like a statue in an ancient temple, he can become a seat for the divine to occupy and transform.

The telestic art (from *télos* – "completion" or "perfection") is the consecration and animation of a statue, then inhabited by a god dwelling in the statue while remaining in the empyrean realm. This is why the temple compound is the *tenemos* – the estate of the god. Oracles and statues are both purified vehicles; the practitioner of Mystery rites may too be a vehicle.

Both the Mysteries and Tantra lead to *télos* – they both channel gods as a vehicle to liberation. Places have the same possibility, and the Telesteria of the Mystery Cults were created specifically for the telestic art. While these are in ruins at both Eleusís and Samothráki, a seeker may still gain much from visiting these sites.

At the Sanctuary of the Great Gods an ancient initiate walked through a primal landscape (mountain and spring on an island in the sea). He entered the Telesterion after passing statues of winged *daímones* (Spirits) and flaming torches. Then he passed through a gate into the *sanctus sanctorum*. At the altar end, he encountered two pillars entwined with carved snakes and topped with stone carved flames. He passed through the Underworld to Hyperborea, entering a realm of the gods.

Twin serpents ascended these columns on an upward path to a fiery realm of light at the summit. Columns were placed on graves in Ancient Greece as a sign of this ascent of the soul. Herakles (who was initiated into the Samothrákian Mysteries) established his Pillars at the world's edge; the aphorism *nōn plūs ultra* was said by Romans to have been inscribed on them. The Samothrákian twin snake fire pillars also indicate there is "nothing beyond here" – that a totality of understanding was represented.

In Iámblikhos' *On the Mysteries*, the Theurgist not only connects the Mysteries to Neoplatonic Therurgy, but also describes gods, archangels, angels, *daímones*, and heroes. All are characterised by light of different qualities. The lower orders are depicted by levels of darkness, heroes are represented with fire, and gods are so bright they make the sun invisible.

The Theurgic ritual involved Apollonian purification of the soul through ablution or lustration. Then an invocation in ancient ritual language served as watchword or key to passing through the veils of supercelestial realms to enter into direct Divine Presence. The transcendent does not receive a soul until it remembers the pure token (a ritual password) it was given to ascend into the centre of divine light.

Before the revelation of light, an initiate must die to the things of this earth. It is a period of ritual death (symbolised by a descent at Eleusís of Persephónē and Dēmétēr into the Underworld); it is the descent of soul into incarnation on this material world. During ritual death one sees phantasms: attachments and aversions to material existence. This is a period of doubleness with a fear of separation and yearning for something higher. After ritual death, an initiate is no longer capable of being trapped as a "shade" in the Underworld, as he has experienced transcendent light – he has witnessed divine illumination. Instead he enters Elysion, the Isles of the Blessed, or Hyperborea as a dweller in light.

The initiate is lost in the darkness of this material world, but through telestic efforts frees his pneumatic vehicle – which he purifies with divine fire – and is guided by the god to the realm of light. There he is reunited with his celestial twin to form a being of pure light. Such a person may become reincarnated on earth as a source of illumination for others, like a bodhisattva in the Eastern tradition.

This is the *Great Work* of the Mystery tradition, preserved through Theurgists who labelled their efforts a continuation of these Mysteries. Recognising an ascent of confessional Christianity, Neoplatonists preserved the Mystery tradition in their writings so it could live on. They understood their work was not necessarily for their time.

Paganism likewise was an exoteric reflex of the esoteric Mysteries. Behind particular gods, goddesses, and their ministers lies an archaic religion that is forebear to European spiritual customs. To this point, the "Chaldean" lineage combined Graeco-Roman esotericism with a deeper Indo-European religious tradition.

In many regards Buddhism also offers keys to understanding the archaic European tradition, as they share ancient origins. That East and West have a common root was recognised by Greeks who contacted India, and Graeco-Buddhism flourished with Alexander's successors. Ancient Greek tradition has at its heart a Self-transcendence comparable to Buddhism, just in different phraseology. Both the Greek Mysteries and Tantrism (of Buddhist and Hindu varieties) reflect a Religion of Light. Platonists and Buddhists provide a hidden map for exploring nature's primal reality once plotted out by Mystery traditions.

The Mysteries remind us who we really are. They persist from an epoch prior to the overlay of Abrahamic faiths. More still, this is a timeless tradition surpassing temporality to access a pristine, original, ever-present state.

At Samothráki one ascends a mountain to the pole. It is a portal to the Spiritual North, land of Eternal Light eclipsing darkness, beyond duality. A seeker is introduced to the twin lights, meeting his divine companion or *daímon*. He is oriented to the North and the Twin Serpents (*kerykeion*).

The initiate passes through terror and confusion. A divine light dawns and he is admitted to its shining realm. He sees sacred visions. He is "sealed" and no longer subject to the suffering of this world. He is given means to navigate the spiritual journey of life.

The illuminating experience is above dogmatism – beyond faith and reason. It is direct and serene cognition of the transcendent. Dying before death and resurrected into Empyrean Light, a seeker comes to know the gods by means of becoming godlike himself. He knows his own divinity and returns to Hyperborea.

Hyperborea is a hidden land accessible only to the worthy in this fallen age. It belongs to those who find a way there.

Part III: The Heroic Initiate

η λατρεία του λύκου

The Wolf Cult

The Mysteries are degenerated and transformed rites of the Wolf Cult. Indo-European warriors saw the wolf as their totemic animal as it embodied their characteristics. Descendants of these ancient steppe nomads, Greeks held the wolf in high esteem. In his zoological works, Aristotle lauds the wolf as *agrios* (fierce), *epíboulos* (cunning), and *gennaíos* (nobly bred). These traits were also required of a warrior elite.

The wolf was their emblem because it was warlike and aristocratic. Wolves hunt as a pack and are social and loyal, so they are emblematic of the group. A lone wolf is dangerous and treacherous. The lion, also a noble animal, was seen as the totem of the single hero, like Herakles.

Wolves are valorous and intelligent with an enterprising spirit. They can go without food and endure cold. The Greeks saw they hunted with intelligence and were able to operate under hardship. Greeks likewise believed that wolves comprehended a relationship between hunting and warfare.

Wolves are also crepuscular hunters: they hunt in the daylight of dawn and dusk, unlike a fox or other predators in the Greek world, which hunted at night. Daylight hunting was seen as a noble trait. The wolf has amber eyes, which can see in strong light.

The children of Helios (the Sun God) are recognisable in Greek myth from their amber eyes, connecting a wolf to the sun. The wolf is also connected to fire. Like the warrior, it has fiery breath, fiery eyes, and fiery rage (*lyssā*).

The wolf is, above all, a wind animal. It is swift like the wind, howling through mountains like the haunting sound of the *aulos* (flute) before initiatory rites.

Greeks never lost contact with their wolfish roots. The first Greeks were said to live in Arkadia ("Bear Land"), which is the location of Mount Lykaion ("Wolf Mountain"). Wolf names are particularly common in Arkadia. Arkadians were the first of the Greek people to enter Greece, and their ancestor Arkas ("Bear") was a son of Zeus Lykaios. Close by, the oldest continually settled town of Argos in the Argolis issued their first coins in the 8th century BCE with a wolf-head device used through the ages.

Lykos' Wood in Messenia was where Lykos ("wolf") initiated people into the mysteries. The Lykeion (Lyceum) in Athens is supposedly named for Lykos son of Pandion, but was part of a set of monuments with wolfish connections including the sanctuary of Herakles at Kynosarges ("white dog" or "swift dog") and a place called Alopkai ("vixens"). The notable classical scholar Jane Harrison called them *a very nest of totemic remembrances.*

Five gods have wolfish aspects – all are connected to secret initiatory rites. Zeus Lykaios presided over the wolf ritual on Mount Lykaion. Men who entered his sanctuary could become a werewolf for nine years, after which they were able to return to human form and back into society. Hermês – a god with a wind aspect like the Indo-Aryan god Vayu – is a psychopomp that conducts souls of the dead to the Underworld. He is a wolf with the epithet Argeiphontes, as he slays Argos the neatherd so Zeus can lie with Io.

While more commonly connected to the bear (another Hyperborean totem), Artemis is also called Lykaia, the she-wolf. She is responsible for the initiation of young "bears" in the female rites at Brauron, as well as the leader of the Greek *Wild Hunt*. Two other gods have wolf incarnations that are most pertinent to Orphic rites. Dionysos is called Lykos at Delphoi, and his tomb is in the temple of his older brother Apollon.

Hermês, Artemis, Dionysos, and Apollon are all children of Zeus, inheriting his wolf nature. Of them all, Apollon is a wolf par excellence; he is Apollon Lykeios: Apollon the Wolf Master. He is god of the wolf wind, a fructifying wind that ripens crops and men.

Young men enter the Underworld as the Wolf Dionysos, assisted by Hermês the Wolf. They emerge after undergoing a trial of initiation, reborn under auspices of Apollon as Master of the Wolf. This distant memory in part survived into Greece's Classical era as two major Athenian festivals. The *Anthesteria* was a spring ghost festival of Dionysos where spirits of ancestral dead were feasted, and the *Thargelia* a summer/autumn "first-fruits" harvest festival of Apollon.

During the *Anthesteria*, ancestor spirits rose on the first day from the Underworld, the *Pithoigia* ("Jar Opening"). While the Athenians had forgotten the original meaning and associated it only with opening Dionysian wine jars, it originally meant the unsealing of graves (ancients buried their dead in pots). In this way the doors of Hảídês were opened.

Next came the *Khoes* ("Cups"), where people drank and made libations. This is a funeral offering to young male initiates who ritually died. The next day was *Oi Khytroi* ("The Pots"). This was originally a reference to sinkholes in the earth. It was where wolves lived and an entrance to the Underworld specifically associated with Apollon.

The young noble men were the original *Kēres* ("dooms" – a kind of spirit) who are banished on the *Khytroi*, not spirits of ancestral dead. They were like other wolf initiates in *Wild Hunt* traditions of Europe: an army of the dead. After wine-fuelled melancholy, initiates embark on their wilderness initiation.

Sacrifice is made to Hermês, conductor of the dead. With his *rhabdos* ("wand") and not his *kerykeion* ("herald's staff"), he leads these wolves into the Underworld. From there they return as men initiated into the Apollonian Wolf Cult.

This was also still present in the Roman *Lupercalia*, where in February the *Luperci* (Wolves) purified the earth with strips of skin. The month of February is named after *februum* – an object used to purge the soul. As the Wolf Cult purifies the earth, it is only right that the purifying god Apollon presides over this task.

After the *Anthesterion* (February) rites of Dionysos, Lord of the Souls of the Dead, a period of three months passed before the Thargelia commenced in May/June. The ancient month of *Thargelion* is sacred to Apollon. At the *Thargelia*, the *Eiresone* – an olive branch twined with white or purple wool and hung with first fruits – was fastened over the door at the temple of Apollon. All first fruits were offered to the god with powers of the fructifying wind: the *pneuma* (Spirit/breath). This originally heralded the return of those young men who had received a *palingenesia* ("spiritual rebirth").

The original fruits were these young men. The youth goes into the underworld as a wolf, emerging as a werewolf: a man in control of his Wolf Spirit. Hermês, god of twilight, takes them into darkness where they encounter Dionysos, god of night. They return with Apollon of the predawn light.

Ο Ορφέας ο μύστης του λύκου

Orpheus the Wolf Initiator

Orpheus eventually became the figure known to late antiquity. However, an examination of his attributes reveals an older form that degenerated over time. Originally, he was a Northern initiator into the Hyperborean Wolf Cult.

Orpheus showed the way in his own story as he ceased to be a wolf and honoured the master of the wolf, graduating from an immature youth of Dionysos to the fully-matured Wolf Warrior of Apollon. This is why he climbed the mountain to greet the dawn like a wolf: he finished the nocturnal rites and awaited the light of dawn. His death allowed him to shed his mortal body and release the divinity within. This is why Dionysos sent the Mainades to tear Orpheus asunder as the former had been rent by the Titans.

Orpheus is the youth hunter archetype. He is the virginal Apollonian Wolf Warrior, the Black Hunter, the *ephēbos* (youth warrior) who lives in the forest. He is more in the vein of Artemis' favourite Hippolytos – the youth who spurns women and prefers the hunt – than a savage wolf of Dionysos. Orphism is linked explicitly to the wilderness and wild living in its most ancient form. Significantly, his listening company in the written and monumental testimonies is made up of men to whom the wild mountain landscape really belongs.

The name "Orpheus" means "Dark One" (*orphē* – "darkness of the night"). The philosopher Herakleitos was also called "Dark One" as he was "difficult to understand" but in reference to Orpheus it carries the meaning "adapted to the night." The mythological name Kelainos, "Dark One," usually appears in a genealogy of Mystery founders.

The usage of this name in Mystery cults testifies to a fact that male maturation ceremonies involving initiation of young men (who first lived as young wolves in the bush, kept away from the opposite sex, and practiced fasting) were once also widespread in Greece as well in other parts of the Indo-European diaspora. A mythical initiator's name with meaning "Dark One" fits ordinations taking place in the wilderness at night. Orpheus is the Dark Initiator of Wolf Warriors in the forest; this is later corrupted into the Orphic religion. It is why Orpheus shares traits with Apollon, but is also Dionysian.

Etymology alone is not the only evidence of this role, but the figure of Orpheus himself and what he embodies paints a picture of a pre-Orphic initiation in the pre-literary stage of Orphism. Orpheus embodies an idea of initiation transforming even the wildest creatures, animals, and men living in the wilderness. He does this not through powers of grain and consecrated friendship with the goddesses of Eleusís, but something young men experienced in wild nature, staying among themselves to the exclusion of all female beings.

These young male initiates discovered the essential through song and music, which liberated them from the bloody savagery of their wolfish life. It was a powerful spiritual and mythological experience, giving a deeper meaning to the ceremony of transition from immaturity to manhood. While the *Theológos* of this mythologem sang and played the lyre he was no mere singer, poet, or *kitharode*: he was the Wolf Cult initiator.

The "animals of Orpheus" who were "drawn to his music like the souls of the dead" were not originally exclusively human. Other animals of the forest also belonged to Orpheus as elements of his milieu, but wolves are particularly his companions. Orpheus is attested to be Apollonian; the Roman poet Ovid calls Orpheus *"Vates Apollineus"* (bard or prophet of Apollon). The Orpheus vase from Geta by the Orpheus Painter also depicts the god playing for Thrakians in fox pelts (closely related to wolves in the ancient mind).

The "wolfish" Lykomidai clan chanted the hymns of Orpheus and seem to have particularly revered Apollon. The Delphic legend connecting Lykos with Apollon Lykeios also shows how wolves belong to Apollon not only mythologically as a form of expression and attribute; Wolves belong to him principally on a level of cultic realisation in a proto-Orphic initiation (implying an early, pre-literary stage of Orphism itself). Orpheus belongs to a circle of Apollon religion: ancient sources about direct or indirect descent from Apollon prove original his intimate relationship with this "pure" and "purifying" god.

That the Thrakian Mainades tear him apart in their Dionysian madness is no reason to deny belief in ancient reports attributing to him a founding role in the Dionysian cult, or participation in Dionysian rites. He is both Dionysian and Apollonian, as both gods are pivotal in Wolf Cult initiations. Orpheus' *katabasis* (Underworld descent) is early in the tradition, connecting him with Dionysos and Hermês as well as Apollon.

Women originally had no place in Orphic Mysteries, because these were Mysteries of the Hyperborean Wolf Cult. Orpheus initiates men into an ancient Hyperborean tradition, singing the cosmogony to instruct these young wolves. This individual liberation does not require formal dogma, just the guidance of an initiator who opens the doors of perception, allowing an initiate to gain realisation. The power of Orpheus' lyre softens hearts of warriors and tames wild beasts into a peaceful Apollonian trance.

The Orphic current is most ancient; it is that of the Hyperborean Wolf Cult. It predates the polarisation of the Apollonian and Dionysian. Apollon is the celestial, Dionysos the chthonic, and Hermês a mediator between the two. In this regard Orpheus acts as Hermês: guide of souls and crux that connects celestial and chthonic impulses.

Apollon is the song, Hermês the words: this is the communication and transmission of mythos. Much as Odin – who Romans identified with Mercury (Hermês) – is responsible for both poetry and Wolf Warriors in the Germanic tradition, the bardic figure of Orpheus is also a magician-shaman who prepares warriors.

Ο Διόνυσος ο Λύκος

Dionysos the Wolf

Dionysos is associated in later antiquity with the frenzied women of his cult: the Mainades. This was not his original retinue. In the Kretan rites, he was associated with warriors.

This is his proper following, as he originally instilled a wolfish frenzy akin to the berserk state of the Germanic *ulfheðinn*. He is the wolf of primaeval return: a reversion to pure chaos in the beginning before order was created. He is the shining Orphic god Phanes resurrected twice with wild traits – a hero-god and divine ancestor of man.

Dionysos-Lykos is the divine wolf spark within the warrior. His power must be harnessed but never allowed to take full and permanent possession of the whole.

Dionysos is the wild Thrakian god in the wilderness. There, the young Wolf Cult initiates go to learn the mysteries. He is a vehicle, via Hermês, to reach the Apollonian mastery of the Self.

Dionysos is Bakkheos, the god who awakens holy madness. The aim of the revelry of the Bakkhantes was to enter into an ecstatic state of spiritual spontaneity or energised enthusiasm. After rending animals apart in the wilderness, Dionysos appeared to them as a bull. Their ultimate aim was union with the god to become themselves a *Bakkhos*.

His original warrior retinue danced with fire to greet the first rising of the Dog Star in high summer. This fire was transformed into a Dionysian "pure light of high summer," the "light of Zeus." The Roman poet Lucanus says, *"Fire is a Dionysian weapon."*

The fire was then placed in the hand of the deity, who was given a procession to cries of "Iakkhos" (Dionysos the torch bearer). This rite negated the Dog Star's ill effect and brought bountiful harvest. It is why the figure of Iakkhos – the light-bringing star of nocturnal mysteries – was incorporated into the Eleusinian Mysteries. He is allied closely with his brother Apollon.

Legend has the figure of Melámpous (seer of Pylos) as regulator of the Dionysian religion. He, like Orpheus, is an Apollonian figure: "Apollon favoured him especially." Apollon was in a particularly close alliance with his brother at Delphoi. While Apollon was in Hyperborea during the winter months, the *Thyiades* of Dionysos rushed over mountains into the Korykian cave, and priests of Apollon held secret rites at the tomb of Dionysos in the temple of Apollon.

The front pediment of the temple depicted Apollon, and the rear Dionysos. Both gods shared in each other's festivals at Delphoi. It was a meeting place of the two divinities who were never in conflict with each other in the ancient world.

Apollon was an intruder at Dephoi in all myths associated with the site. Most commonly he kills Delphyne or Python, representing perhaps the ancient goddesses Gaîa and Themis who ruled over the site previously. The Scholiast of Argonautika states, *"Among the older deities he supplanted there, the name Dionysos also occurred."*

Dionysos was the *prómantis* (oracle) of Nyx at Delphoi. It was the temple of Dionysos Nyktélios (Nocturnal Dionysos). This connection to Phanes and Nyx is revealed in the Orphic initiation.

Dionysos' nighttime aspect is the counterpart of Apollon's daytime aspect. In areas ruled over by Apollon, Dionysos retained his nocturnal wildness (mountain worship). Elsewhere he was tamed and urbanised. When he is with Apollon, Dionysos' true character emerges.

It was in winter, when Apollon was with his favoured people in the Far North, that Dionysos reigned in Delphoi. He represents eternal undying life (*bios*). His symbols are the ivy and the pine cone, as they do not die in winter. His tomb was in Delphoi, but he still lived.

The immortal wolf lives on; it is merely temporarily entombed in the body. The wolf is buried in the tomb the same way as in Orphic thought that a soul is buried in the *sema* ("tomb") of the *soma* ("body"). In this sense the initiate knows Dionysos is inside, Hermês is close by, and Apollon is far away.

Dionysos' ecstatic Wolf Cult berserk element is enduring. The ecstatic *mantikê* (divination) remained at Delphoi after it was subordinated to Apollon. This is because Apollon is not disconnected from a state of "enthusiasm" or "possession."

The Delphic Oracle's pronouncements were induced by vapours from a chasm: the "wind" or "Spirit." Apollon's wolf wind filled the priestess with the god (*entheos*), putting her in a state of divine Dionysian madness.

Dionysos is linked with the hero in myth. In the Greek hero cult, the deceased hero is represented as a snake. The hero becomes a snake after death as shown on imagery of heroic tombs. Dionysos' Kretan rites had a snake in the mystery casket.

Dionysos is a hero-god, a late addition to the Olympic pantheon with characteristics of a hero. Heroes were said to enjoy a Dionysian existence in Elysion after they died. Over time the snake became only an emblem of the hero, rather than the actual hero. The double axe is also a symbol of Dionysos; it is a battle weapon used to slay the Dionysian bull during sacrifice.

Dionysos is present for the early part of a warrior's training, when he is very young. The retinue of Dionysos is made up of satyrs and kentaurs – both "wild men." The kentaur Kheírōn raised and trained both Akhilleús and Iásōn in the wild like a feral animal. This represents an early phase in the training of a Wolf Warrior.

First he must learn to be ferocious. He must be savage so he is able to build his battle fury. Later, the wolf is initiated and must be tamed. This is represented by the myth of the Apollonian Lapithes and Theseus defeating unruly kentaurs who became frenzied on wine at a wedding feast.

Dionysos is the dark realm of becoming. Apollon is the bright realm of Being. The light upper realm of the Spirit has its counterfoil in the dark earthly realm of the soul.

Ὁ Ἀπόλλων Λύκειος

Apollon the Wolf God

Apollon and Dionysos are reflections of the divine "twins" – aspects of the same *Theos* (God). Both lived at Delphoi and were not in opposition to each other. The tomb of Dionysos Lykos is in the temple of Apollon at Dephoi and statues of two kouroi (youths), normally associated with the Díoskouroi ("Zeus' Boys") were also found at the sanctuary. Normally the pair are seen as Kástor and Polydeúkes, but they could also equally represent Apollon and Dionysos.

The relationship of these two deities is close knit. Dionysos is Lykos the Wolf, sacrificed by the Titans so that parts of him could become embedded within man. Apollon Lykeios is "Master of the Wolf;" this "Wolfish Apollon" is the god who controls the wolf instinct, allowing a mature initiate to operate within society. Hence the Delphic command to "Know Thyself" – know that thou art man (not wolf).

Both Dionysos Lykos and Apollon Lykeios require ecstatic discovery. This was clear at Delphoi with its entheogenic issuance of oracles via the channel of a *mantis* ("oracle"). It is particularly linked to Apollon, as the mantis entered into an ecstatic state through vapours issuing forth from a chasm.

The sibyl in Virgil's *Aeneid* "breathes in" Apollon. He approaches her as a wind and fills her with convulsions of thunder and lightning. His wind fills her and animates her. Wind, Spirit, and breath are all *pneuma* in Greek. Apollon as the Wolf God is associated with "winds" pouring out of caves. The North Wind Boreas abided in a cave near Hyperborea, and wolves were specifically connected to winds and caves.

Delphoi is a Wolf Cult site, as it is also the place of a dragon slaying myth. This type of myth is explicitly connected to the Wolf Cult across the Indo-European diaspora. In the Delphic myth, Apollon conquers the serpentine son of Gaîa (Python or Drakōn), constructing his temple on its tomb. This is none other than the grave of Chthonic Dionysos. Serpent and dragon are seen as forms of the wolf in the broader mythos; both dragon and wolf are spirits of the storm.

The Dragon Slayer is he who subdues his inner wolf. Just as in the Vedic mythos where the conquered Vṛtrá becomes Soma, so the conquered Python becomes Dionysos. The dragon-wolf obstacle is overcome and made into a source of power for the Wolf Warrior. Apollon similarly conquered a local chthonic deity Hyakinthos at Sparta, absorbing the god into himself – the subterranean is yoked by the celestial.

In the Orphic mythos, Zeus strikes the Titans down with his thunderbolt after they kill Dionysos. In Greek myth, heroes are often struck by Zeus' thunderbolt, not to kill them, but to translate them to another plane – a higher existence outside the visible world. When Zeus throws his thunderbolt at the Titans, this represents the translation to a higher realm of both the Titans and Dionysos.

The Wolf is killed by the titanic elements within the initiate. He then experiences the thunderbolt conversion to a higher plane of existence. Apollon takes the body parts of Dionysos to Delphoi so that the Wolf remains a source of power.

At the Russian Bronze Age site of Krasnosamarskoe, evidence of winter Wolf Rites suggests the young warrior initiate took his wolf (dog) with him and slayed it, merging canine and master into a more powerful combination of the two. This remarkable find confirms much of what is encoded in the Greek mythological record.

The wolfish sacrifice has a reflection in Delphoi. Weapons were not allowed in temple precincts – everyone had to be unarmed. Sacrificial implements, specifically the sacrificial knife and axe, were excluded from this as they were no longer weapons but instruments. No man fought with a *makhaira* (knife), only a *xiphos* (sword). When knives were drawn it was no longer combat between men, but battle between wild beasts who claw and bite. The knife was associated with butchery.

The knife was a weapon of the *epheboi,* and Spartan *kryptai* (elite youth warriors with lycanthropic traits) could only carry a knife when on their ritual raids of the enslaved Helot population. The wolf carries the *makhaira* as it symbolises his teeth. The phrase "each knife can conceal a wolf" was well-known in Ancient Greece.

Knives could be carried into temple precincts as they were linked to the sacrifice. Apollon at Delphoi was known as "prince of sacrificers;" when someone went to sacrifice at Delphoi, Delphinian men surrounded the altar, each carrying a knife. After the priest conducted the sacrifice, each man descended on the carcass and carved off a piece like a pack of wolves. Under the gaze of Lord Apollon, the Wolfpack gathered to form the circle of death.

The sacrifice itself as a Panhellenic institution is linked closely to the wolfish circle of death. The animal consisted of three parts: *krea* (meat), *ostia* (bones), and *splankhna* (viscera). Before distributing meat to a broader sacrificial community during the "*krea* phase," the thighbones were cut out and wrapped in fat. These were cast into a sacrificial fire as the *meria* (gods' share), which is also called the *thúein* (burned part) as opposed to the *hiereúein* (eaten part).

Then the *splankhna* were cooked on the same sacrificial flame. The "eaters of the *splankhna*" were a restricted circle limited to sacrificial elite. This "*splankhna* phase" (eating the viscera) was a maximum participation in the sacrifice by an inner circle of men.

The *thúein* always refers to an Olympian sacrifice which is seen as white, bright, above in the upper air: a beneficent tending sacrifice. The *henagízein* is a sacrifice to the dead and those below. This was a chthonic holocaustal blood sacrifice representing black, dark, below in the murk, malignance: a sacrifice of riddance. Offerings to the dead were at dusk, and to Ouranians (Olympians) at dawn. The victim slain for chthonic purification is called *sphagion* ("a thing slaughtered"). *Sphagion* is always the term used for human victims, so the animal is a substitute for human sacrifice.

While they are *ephēboi*, Wolf Initiates cannot partake in a *thúein* sacrifice. They can only do so once they have conquered their wolf and reentered society as fully fledged mature warriors: Wolves of Apollon. When they are full adult members of the warrior caste, they have maximum participation in the sacrifice, becoming "eaters of the *splankhna*." Wool fillets are worn for sacrifice, which explains the prohibition on wool by later Orphics.

Apollon is the purifying god, a trait giving him a chthonic aspect. Later Orphism was fixated on ritual purification, linking it to the Apollonian Wolf Cult. Ritual purification after pollution does not distinguish between major and minor pollutions.

Pollution is pollution, whether touching offerings to the dead, coming into contact with a pregnant woman, or murder. Whether a killing was intentional or not and whether the killer shows remorse or not is irrelevant. Purification is purification. Different ritual acts were performed for different kinds of pollution, but they were all effective at purifying the individual.

Apollon is a dragon slayer and representative of the power of a younger generation of Olympians. He is god of the *ephēboi*: young werewolf warriors. A statue of a wolf stood at the altar in front of the main temple at Delphoi. His name suggests that he is an initiatory god.

Apollon was known as Apellon in Sparta, a name that was used more broadly in pre-Homeric Greek. This is linked to the *apellai* – tribal fraternal gatherings and rites of initiation. He was called Apellon the Ephēbos and Apollon *Akersekomas* ("of the unshorn hair"). Initiates dedicated their forelocks at Delphoi to mark their transition into manhood. Many societies call the adolescent bands the "stranger wolves." Apollon Lykaios is not god of a fugitive or lone wolf, but only the wolf band.

Apollon inherited his wolf epithet from Zeus. Zeus Lykaios (originally Lykeios) was the presiding wolf god on Mount Lykaion in Arkadia, also a Wolf Cult initiation site. The only other gods with this epithet are Artemis Lykeia and Pan Lykeios.

Pan is son of Hermês, but sometimes considered a child of Apollon. He is really a form of Hermês as "watcher," and also related to Dionysos in his form of a Satyr. Both Pan and Apollon carry the epithet Nomios ("protector of the flocks") – being that of the wolf god. The wolf can protect or kill the multitude.

The hero Lykos was protector of the law courts in Athens. He is also said to have built the Lykeion, which functioned as the law court and had a wolf statue in front. This was the temple of Apollon Lykeios.

Lykōreia, an oracular site of Apollon near Delphoi, was older than Delphoi itself. The winds that blew across Mount Parnassos were thought to be wolf winds of Apollon. Since time immemorial, Apollon and wolves were associated with that area and the Korykian cave.

Apollon also bears the epithet Lykēgenēs ("Wolf-born"). After becoming pregnant by Zeus, Apollon and Artemis' mother Leto came to Delos after her sojourn in Hyperborea. For twelve days she took on wolf form (she-wolves whelp for twelve days). Leto was in this form when she bore both Apollon and Artemis, so Apollon is thus born of the wolf. Roman poet and grammarian Servius says a wolf brought Apollon a laurel crown from Tempe after his victory over the serpent. The wolf is associated from the outset with Apollon.

Apollon, in his wolfish aspect, is connected particularly to light and wind. Macrobius tells us in his *Saturnalia* that *"the ancient Greeks called the first light that appears before sunrise lykē from tó leukón ("brightness"). Today too that time of day is called lykóphos ("wolf light")."* The word *lykē* derives from *lykos* ("wolf"). Macrobius states that the Latin word *lux* directly comes from *lykē*.

The sun in the *Thebaid* of Statius is called *lykos*. The wolf is related to sun and light as the wolf is a crepuscular animal. It is most active as the sun rises and sets. Apollon is god of the predawn light, and Hermês of twilight.

Wind is like a wolf in that it can harm or help. The fructifying wind brings ripeness to crops, whereas storm winds destroy all in their path. This power of a wolf in the wind is one of the first stories we learn as children to this day. In the tale of *The Three Little Pigs* a "Big Bad Wolf" huffs, puffs, and blows their house down.

The dangerous storm winds are more properly associated with Zeus, who passed on his wind element to his son Apollon. The Wolf Wind of Apollon is a fructifying good wind. According to mythologist Walter W. Kelly, Apollon and Zeus are cognate to Vedic Rudra and Indra respectively. Indra is a storm god and Rudra is the "Roarer," an apt name for a wind deity.

Apollon and Rudra also share another characteristic in common: Rudra is sometimes called Rudra Vaṅku ("Rudra the Staggerer);" Apollon Loxias ("Apollon who proceeds athwart") is cognate with this. The names both indicate zigzag walking – loping like the wolf. Turbulent storm winds are also associated with Apollon, just as Rudra is father of storm winds (the Maruts). Storm winds break down doors and rip off roofs, opening previously closed paths of consciousness; as much as fructifying winds, storm winds bring change and development.

Winds issue forth from caves in the ancient mind. Caves are wolf lairs, hence the pan-Indo-European concept of a wind-wolf. This makes the wind something of an invisible realm. Both wolf and wind are messengers from the otherworld. This connects wind to Hermês (herald of gods) as well as his Vedic counterpart Vayu. Both Hermês and Vayu are ambiguous figures, embodying beneficial and ambiguous characteristics, much like wind and the wolf.

The mania of Dionysos similarly comes from the invisible realm. So too does the "breath of Apollon" that poured out of the chasm at Delphoi, filling the *mantis* with vapours. The breath of Apollon transported the initiate Aristéas close to Hyperborea when he was *phoibólamtos yenómenos* ("possessed by Phoibos").

Entry into a cave by an invisible Wolf Initiate was part of the mythos. The invisibility aspect is a feature of the wolf and by extension Wolf Warriors. The sinkhole in particular was seen as an entrance to the Underworld, a place where winds issue forth, and an abode of wolves. The wolf's maw represents death and rebirth; in this regard, Apollon as Wolf God is connected to the Underworld.

In the story of Perseus, the hero dons the *Aïdos kynéē* ("dog-skin of Hãïdēs"), a wolf skin cap rendering him invisible so he can slay the gorgon Medousa. The dead are invisible, and Wolves of Apollon are invisible because they are ritually dead. They enter into the Underworld and return to the living after they take off the wolfskin and reenter society.

In the summer in Greece, rivers dry up leaving sinkholes open to issue gases. Water is associated with the lunar bull personified by Dionysos. He enters the Underworld through a sinkhole as the waters enter Hãîdēs. Solar wind issues forth when lunar water enters. The gas from chasms can be ignited by lightning and create underground fire.

The wolf is wind and fire. This is a reflection of the entry of an initiate into the Underworld to retrieve a light. He enters in a Dionysian fashion and exits with an Apollonian character.

Theseus in the Labyrinth is a Wolf Warrior in the Underworld. In addition to Orpheus, Herakles and Odysseus all enter the Underworld emulating Apollon following his killing of Python. Apollon had to work for Admētos to atone for spilling the blood of Python. Admētos ("Untamed") is an epithet of Hãîdēs. Thus Apollon had to enter the Underworld and purify himself of accrued pollution.

Orpheus made his descent into the Underworld originally as a wolf cultist. He then initiated others into the Wolf Cult. This later became the broader tantric Mystery tradition of Greece.

At Mount Soracte in Magna Grecia, Apollon was worshipped as Soranus Pater (Etruscan: Śuri), a Lord of the Underworld. The priests of Soranus were called *Hirpi Sorani* ("Wolves of Soranus" – from Sabine: *hirpus* "wolf"). Apollon as

Wolf God is responsible for guiding Wolf Cultists through an initiation of the Underworld. The werewolf penetrates this unseen world: the Underworld which is Chaos. It contains all possibilities, both good and evil. Thus the wolf band can choose to be good, working for society while removed from it, or bad, never able to return.

Lykeios can overcome the ritual death of a wolf initiation. Lykos can never become human again, remaining a permanent wolf. He cannot enter the city; wolves cannot found cities or lead governments, or they fall into tyranny. This is the wolf that is not tamed by Lykeios.

Apollon Lykeios subjugates Dionysos Lykos and darkness. He is light heralding the coming of dawn. God of the mature reasoned warrior, Apollon subjugates and controls the high spirits and ravenous appetites of the young represented by Dionysos. Young warriors enter the Wolf Cult as Dionysos, but wind wolf Apollon matures them as the wolf wind ripens grain.

The wind specifically connected to Apollon Lykeios is the fructifying wind that ripens crops. This is one reason why Wolf Cultists throughout the Indo-European diaspora conducted fertility rituals on behalf of society. Aside from the Athenian *Thargelia* (First Fruits) on Delos, Apollon was father of Oinō, Spermō, and Elais (the *oinotopoi* – "wine-growers") being wine, grain, and olive. Hyperboreans offered first fruits at the *Thargelia* of Delos, sending them from their northern home to this small Greek island sacred to Apollon.

In Dorian areas, the *Karneia*, an important festival of Apollon, was a celebration of bringing in the grapes. Observed three months after the *Thargelia* at Eleusís, the *Karneia* was sacred to Apollon Pythios, god of prophesy. The *Karneia* honoured the death of the prophet Karnos; men of Sparta lived in groups of nine in huts of greenery in memory of the military formations of the Heraklidai ("Children of Herakles"), who Karnos led back to their Peloponnesian home. Karnos was "an apparition of Apollon" who was murdered by Hippōtes at Naupaktos, just before the Heraklidai entered their ancestral homeland. This was a human sacrifice to benefit the Dorian people.

Across Europe the fructifying wind is related to the wolf. The grain rust known as ergot is particularly important in this ripening function. In many parts of Europe ergot is called "wolf." The LSD-containing ergot of barley may have been what was in the *kykeôn* at Eleusís.

Apollon is a red god of grain rust with the epithet Erythibios ("of the cereal rust"). Romans worshipped him under this aspect as Apollo Robigus. During the *Robigalia* festival in April, they sacrificed a dog (a substitute for a wolf) – a reflex of the sacrifice performed by confraternities of young men at the rising of Sirius (Dog Star) in the "dog days" of September.

Zephyros is primarily the wolf-wind in this function as it is the westerly fructifying wind. The fructifying wind does not only ripen crops, but also men. It matures the youth into fully-fledged Wolf Warriors as well as bringing the human Spirit to fruition. Apollon as *männerbund* god brings youthful wolves to maturity. This is represented in the Orphic theogony by a wind-born egg from which Phanes-Dionysos hatches.

Thus, the wolf wind of Apollon ripens crops and men. Man is a microcosm and his "inner realm" is also a reflection of the wind's invisible, intangible realm. His Spirit is the wind. The "high spirits" of Homeric heroes – termed *thumós* and *ménos* – are related to the Spirit, in turn ruled over by Apollon.

Boreas is also a purifying northern wolf wind counteracting the poisonous southern wind of summer months. Boreas carried Leto to Delos from Hyperborea where she took on wolf form before giving birth to Apollon and Artemis. Graeco-Roman geographer Stabo quotes Sokrates as saying Boreas' home is *"over the sea, at the ends of the earth and wellsprings of Night, where the heavens open up and the ancient garden of Phoibos is located."* This is Hyperborea in the Far North, home of Apollon.

Boreas' sons, Argonauts Kalais and Zētēs, are Hyperboreans. The Hyperborean maidens Upis, Loxō, and Hekaergē were daughters of Boreas according to Kallimakhos. Among the Hyperboreans, three nine-foot-tall giants, children of Khione (Frost Maiden) and Boreas, and their descendants were priests of Apollon. Boreas has a son Lykourgos ("Wolf Worker"). In winter, while Apollon is in Hyperborea and Dionysos is at Delphoi, the Hyperboreans sacrifice asses to him. Asses are the animal of Dionysos.

Apollon Lykeios is patron of the martial spirit; he is also Master of the Wolf, and of both hidden and manifest. He crosses between worlds, living in both the visible and invisible (Hyperborea is the hidden world – a transcendent realm). He is god of the wolf confraternity (but not wild Wolf Warriors) who makes them mature pillars of society. He guides their energy, since a warrior must be reasoned and sane towards society, but wild and ferocious to his enemies.

Apollon is god of Wolf Warriors even after they are mature. In Euripides' *Rhesos*, he describes Diomedes and Odysseus as wolves on horseback slaying the sleeping Thrakians. They are still wolves, even as fully-fledged warrior nobles.

These warriors have the power to unleash the Dionysian Lykos – a wolf-spark resting in their hearts – when battle begins, but also the ability to control it. Dionysos is the frenzied power of the wolf; Apollon is the power to master it. Only a man who has become the wolf can truly wield this power.

The mature warrior controls the high-spirited youthful fighter. The Apollonian controls Dionysian, but a wolf is always present within. The Noble Wolf protects its pack as well as the "herd" (citizenry), which is why the wolf is a leadership totem. It is also why the Capitoline sanctuary of Rome was guarded by Deus Lucoris: the Wolf God.

φοιβόλαμτος γενόμενος

Possessed by Apollon

Hyperborean shamanic trance journey of one possessed by Apollon is attested in the Ancient Greek record. The *apophoibōmenos* ("frenzy from Phoibos") induced one to be *phoibólyptos* ("seized by Phoibos") or *phoibólamtos yenòmenos* ("possessed by Phoibos"). Pausanias states in his *Description of Greece* 1.34.3: *"Apart from those who suffered Apollonian madness none of the soothsayers in antiquity was a prophet."* Four cases of trance journey in particular are recorded by ancient writers, the most notable being Aristéas of Prokonnesos. All four came to be connected to Pythagóras, and the practice (if not the philosophy) of Pythagoreanism grew through the ideas of these "wise men."

Eighth century BCE philosopher and mystic Hermótimos of Klazomenaí would leave his body for years, bringing back mantic lore and future knowledge from his ecstatic voyages. Betrayed by his wife, the enemies of Hermótimos burned his body while he was away so he could no longer return to the material plane.

The greatest master of this was Epimenídes of Krete, a seventh century BCE philosopher and priest who wrote the now-lost *Orphic Cosmogony* and *Argonautika*. Adherent of the cult of Zeus, he stayed at length on Mount Ida in the cave of Zeus, intercoursing with spirits of the darkness while fasting. He engaged in a long period of ecstasy and returned to the light of day far travelled in "enthusiastic wisdom." Next he journeyed through many lands healing and prophesying, acting as a kathartic priest, expelling *daímonaic* evils from people's past misdeeds. He purified Athens from murdering the followers of Kylon, appeasing their spirits through potent sacrificial rites and secret wisdom. He was remembered across Greece and particularly on Apollon's sacred island of Delos.

Ábaris the Hyperborean was known as an *aithrobátēs* ("aither traveller"). Sent from Hyperborea by Apollon, Ábaris needed no food and passed through many lands dispelling sickness of mind and soul though sacrifice and *epodaí* ("incantations"). He is said to have written several works including a theogony, the *Skythian Oracles*, a book of purifications, and an account of Apollon's visit to Hyperborea.

Carrying a golden arrow as proof of his mission, Ábaris was said to "ride the Arrow of Hyperborean Apollon." The arrow was a vehicle symbolising his trance journeys. According to Porphyry's *Life of Pythagóras* he traversed rivers, seas, and steeps by "walking in the air." This is an ecstatic "journey of the soul." Ábaris met Apollon at Delphoi, obtaining mantic power.

Aristéas of Prokonnesos is the most famous of all Apollon's ecstatics. Claimed also by the later Pythagoreans as one of their great wise men, he is said to have journeyed towards Hyperborea in a trance "possessed by Apollon." Aristéas wrote a poem called the *Arimaspeia* recounting his journey of which only two small fragments remain. One is in the first century CE work *On the Sublime* by Longĩnos, and the other Iōánnēs Tzétzēs' tenth century *Khiliades*.

Maximus of Tyre in the second century CE describes the flight of Aristéas as follows: *"Aristéas recounted how his soul left his body and, flying in the sky, it passed the countries, Greek and others, all the islands, the rivers, the mountains[...] There was a man from Prokonnesos, whose body was lying with hardly apparent signs of life, in a state very close to death; during this time, his soul had left the body and was travelling in the sky as a bird, visiting everything below, the earth, the sea, the rivers, the towns, the peoples[...] then the soul, having come back, reanimated the body, and he recounted the different things the soul had seen and heard."* The bird in question was likely a crow, which is sacred to Apollon.

The longest account that survives is that of Hēródotos in his *Histories* 4.12:

"Aristéas also, the son of Kaystrobios, a native of Prokonnessos, says in the course of his poem that, possessed by Apollon, he reached the Issedonians. Above them dwelt the Arimaspi, men with one eye; still further, the gold-guarding gryphons; and beyond these, the Hyperboreans, whose country extended to the sea. Except the

Hyperboreans, all these nations, beginning with the Arimaspi, continually encroached on their neighbours. Hence it came to pass that the Arimaspi gradually drove the Issedonians from their country, while the Issedonians dispossessed the Skyths; and the Skyths, pressing upon the Kimmerians, who dwelt on the shores of the southern sea, forced them to leave their land.

"The birthplace of Aristéas, the poet who sang of these things, I have already mentioned. I will now relate a tale which I heard concerning him at Prokonnessos and Kyzikos. Aristéas, they said, who belonged to one of the noblest families in the island, had entered one day a fuller's shop, when he suddenly dropped down dead. Hereupon the fuller shut up his shop, and went to tell Aristéas' kindred what had happened. The report of the death had just spread through the town, when a certain Kyzikenian, lately arrived from Artákē, contradicted the rumour, affirming that he had met Aristéas on the road to Kyzikos, and had spoken with him. This man, therefore, strenuously denied the rumour; the relations however proceeded to the fuller's shop with all things necessary for the funeral, intending to carry the body away. But on the shop being opened, no Aristéas was found, either dead or alive. Six years afterwards he reappeared, they told me, in Prokonnessos, and composed the poem which the Greeks now know as the Arimaspeia, after which he disappeared a second time. This is the tale current in the two cities above mentioned.

"What follows I know to have happened to the Metapontines in Italy two hundred and forty years after the second disappearance of Aristéas, as I discovered by calculations I made at Prokonnessos and Metapontum. Aristéas then, as the Metapontines affirm, appeared to

161

them in their own country in person, and ordered them to set up an altar in honour of Apollon, and to place near it a statue to be called that of Aristéas the Prokonnessian. Apollon, he told them, had honoured them alone of the Italiotes with his presence; and he himself accompanied the god at the time, not however in his present form, but in the shape of a raven. Having said so much he vanished. Then the Metapontines sent to Delphoi, and inquired of the god what they were to make of this apparition. The priestess in reply bade them attend to what the spectre said, 'for so it would go best with them.' Thus advised, they did as they had been directed; and there is now a statue bearing the name of Aristéas, close by the image of Apollon in the market-place of Metapontum, with bay trees standing round it. But enough has been said concerning Aristéas.

"With regard to the regions which lie above the country whereof this portion of my history treats, there is no one who possesses any exact knowledge. Not a single person can I find who professes to be acquainted with them by actual observation. Even Aristéas, whom I have just mentioned – even he did not claim in his poem to have got further than the Issedonians, but on his own confession what he related of the regions beyond was hearsay, being the account which the Issedonians gave him of these countries."

Aristéas could harness the magic of *ekstasis*. His soul left his body "seized by Phoibos" and his second Self made itself visible in distant places. Aristéas was possessed by Apollon (filled with the Spirit of the god), who breathed his wind into the man. He was able to travel through time and space on a shamanic trance journey as an attendant of Apollon, flying through the air in the god's chariot. Pliny recounts that the soul of Aristéas was seen leaving his mouth in the form of a raven; thus he was able to travel where and when he wished. The *Arimaspeia* – as we can ascertain from ancient authors – gave a clear description of Aristéas' route North.

Aristéas began his journey in the Greek colony of Prokonnessos on an island near Kyzikos, named after king Kyzikós, a son of Apollon accidentally killed by the Argonauts. The area was part of Phrygia in antiquity and a hub of Apollon worship. He travelled through the land of the Skythians to the Issedonians. Hēródotos says these Issedonians lay beyond the range of the Skythian trade route. According to ancient writers, this was as far as he physically travelled. His poem, however, related the people and lands beyond the Issedonians: the Arimaspians and Hyperboreans.

In *Description of Greece* 1.24.6, Pausanias says: *"Aristéas of Prokonnesos says in his poem that gryphons fight for gold with the Arimaspians who dwell beyond the Issedonians, and that the gold which the gryphons guard is produced by the earth. He says too that the Arimaspians are all one-eyed men from birth, and the gryphons are wild monsters like lions with wings and the beak of an eagle."*

Aristéas is first to talk of the Arimaspians, a word that comes from Iranian, not Greek. These northern men are horse-keeping nomads, rich in cattle, with a single eye. They battle the powerful gryphons in order to steal their gold, which they dig up in order to build their lairs. Kallimakhos, in his *Aítia* (fragment 186.8), calls the Arimaspians *"sons of the Hyperboreans' escort."* He says of the Hyperborean offerings that the men of Dodona *"are the first of the Greeks to receive them from their Arimaspian convoy."*

Following on from Aristéas' disembodied soul journey as a raven, this *gryptomakhia* of the "warlike" Arimaspians became a popular theme in Greek art. Gryphons are Apollonian and often depicted pulling the god's chariot, but their eagle quality also ties them to Zeus. Aiskhýlos in *Prometheus Bound*, has Prometheus give the following advice to the wandering Io: *"Beware the sharp-beaked gryphons, hounds of Zeus that bark not, and the host of the one-eyed Arimaspians, the horsemen who live about Plouton's stream that flows with gold."*

Possibly drawing from Aristéas, both Aiskhýlos and Pindar place gryphons in the northeast immediately after the Graiai and Gorgons. This is contrary to most ancient writers who place the Graiai and Gorgons in the west. Pindar specifically places them near the Hyperboreans.

The Graiai – three blind sisters who share an eye, but know the future – are questioned by the hero Perseus who visits them to discover the way to the Gorgons. On his way back from slaying Medousa, Perseus visits the Hyperboreans. Aiskhýlos describes the Graiai as "swanlike," tying them to Apollon to whom the swan belongs. It also makes their northeastern placement clearer, as it connects their cave to the Rhipaian Mountains marking a boundary to the Hyperborean realm.

According to the *Soûda*, Damastes of Sígeion stated: *"Beyond the Scythians dwell the Issedonians, beyond them the Arimaspi, then there are the Rhipaian Mountains, from which Boreas blows and where there is always snow. Beyond these mountains the country of the Hyperboreans reaches down to the other sea."* *"Rhipe buried in darkness"* is how Sophokles describes it, or to quote Alkman (fragment 59): *"Mountain of Rhipe of the storm blast, blossoming with woods, breast of black night."*

Rhipe, or the Rhipai Mountains are thus in the realm of Nyx (Night), mother of the gods in the ancient Orphic tradition. On the edge of the world, always dark, shrouded by Night and storms and "feathers of snow," they are clearly connected to the goddess Nyx who as a bird lays the cosmic egg in one version of the cosmogony. On this mountain range is a cave of the "swanlike" mantic Graiai, both Apollonian and emanations of a great ancient mother goddess who prophesies to the gods from her cave.

Also on Rhipe is a cave of the North Wind. It is from his cavern that Boreas sends his purifying wind down into the world. Nearby this cave (which Pliny calls *"entrance to the Earth's windpipe"*) the herb called Phrixa is said to grow abundantly by the Tanais River flowing from the mountains. Aiskhýlos calls this *"the spring of Plouton's stream that flows with gold."*

This places the Rhipaian mountains squarely in the Indo-European mythos. In the Iranian tradition, White Haoma grows next to the Cosmic River on the Cosmic Mountain. The Sacred

River is the Milky Way, which the Greek mystic Empedótimos called *"the path of the souls who traverse Hā́idēs in the sky."*

The "Rhipaian Kaukasos" are the mountains Kronos fled from Zeus to after the Titans lost their war with the gods. Kronos is king of the Golden Age, ruling over the Isles of the Blessed. Conflated with the Arctic Ocean, the Kronian Sea was beyond the mountain and a place where Hyperborea was to be found, beyond the "lair of the North Wind."

In the Orphic and Hesiodic iterations of the Argonaut myth, Iásōn sails up the Phasis River (the Phasis Strait) to reach Kolkhís on the shore of Okeanos. According to Mimnermos in the 7th century BCE (Fragment 2.5ff): *"The city of Aiḗtēs, where the rays of the swift Sun rest in a golden store-room, by the lip of Okeanos, whither god-like Iásōn went."* Aiḗtēs, king of Kolkhís, is like Kronos a ruler over a golden land.

This is the Greek echo of Indo-European mythos told among a Wolf Elite: ascend a Holy Mountain surrounded by the Ocean by following a Sacred River past the herb of immortality and beyond the Cavern of the Wind. Beyond this mountain, ruled over by the King of the Golden Age, lies a land of immortals loved by the gods more than any other: the Hyperboreans.

What is especially pertinent about this description is that Asian sources support this mythos. The ancient Chinese *Shānhǎi Jīng* (*Classic of Mountains and Seas*) confirms much of what Aristéas claims including dog-heads, one-eyed men, gryphons, and a cave of the wind. The Mongols talk of a golden mountain in the North that supports the sky called "Sumur" or "Sumer" (the Rhipaian Mountains in the far north are filled with gold). Indic mythology also recognises the Hyperborean people beyond the holy world mountain, calling their land *Utturakuru*.

Hyperborea is Land of the Eternal Sun, Hãidēs in the Sky, and the Isles of the Blessed. This place lies beyond the material realm of gods in an immaterial True North. Neither by ship nor on foot can you find your way to the marvellous assembly of the Hyperboreans. The Spirit must leave the body and see it. Only a true seer, an elite Wolf Cultist, may make this journey.

The Return to Hyperborea – that original *atidevic* state of Being – is not possible for the average man. It is reserved for the few. Only the noble ones can hope to make this cosmic leap. Even fewer can travel between our material *Kosmos* and Hyperborea at will, coming and going as they please. To achieve this is an ultimate goal of the Wolf Initiate.

Once his Spirit has seen Hyperborea, he can aid other noble souls to escape the bonds of the *Kosmos*. Emulating Orpheus, he becomes the *Dark One* illuminating Spirits of men.

το τάντρα του υπερβορείου λύκου

Hyperborean Wolf Tantra

Like the Mysteries that generated from them, initiation into the Wolf Cult has a direct eastern parallel in tantra, which also came from a Northern origin. Tantra is the only method suitable for the Kali Yuga, as ancient ways are not appropriate for men of this time to attain liberation. We must discover a Western tantra of the Mysteries (and Wolf Cult) in order to attain true understanding and make the Return.

The mother-daughter mysteries are a feminine initiation. They appear in the male initiation, but in a diminished role. The revealing of the goddess to women became the Eleusinian and other female, matriarchal Mysteries. Men originally had no place in these Mysteries as they had their own in the Wolf Cult.

As the structure of society broke down from its original aristocratic warrior-led system, the Mysteries devolved into democratic salvation religions and immortality cults for the masses, losing their original character and meaning. Thus the tantra was lost. Both male and female complementary traditions disappeared into the murk of the Age of Iron.

The twofold Wolf Initiation of Orpheus – where he sung the cosmogony to initiate the young wolves – seems lost, but the true Orphic high road of the gods is immortal. What is timeless is always present. The initiate first becomes Lykos, travelling the Wolf Road, initiated first as a wolf and warrior. He dies as a boy and is reborn a wolf.

The path ahead then forks: the initiate may continue on the path of Lykos (remaining forever outside society), or refine and purify his Spirit on the way of Lykeios. He can become the social werewolf, both man and wolf. Here is the true tantric process leading to real rebirth as a potent godlike being who can straddle the worlds.

Orpheus, the lyre-playing initiator, gives harmonious order to the disordered youthful initiates, providing a framework within which to navigate their chaotic existence. He does this through the harmony and vibration of musical notes while offering images with his song that must be understood on an irrational level. Orpheus is a priest of Dionysos because he sings to the irrational ecstatic divine wolf element within; he is a priest of Apollon because he aids the initiates in mastering the chaotic Dionysian. He enables them to control this divinity, allowing them to utilise it without becoming lost to it.

The complete initiate can bring his inner being into harmony, both within his Self and between Self and *Kosmos*. All the *Kosmos* is contained within man: the elements, gods, animals, plants, and powers. He is a true microcosm; he is Zeus swallowing the *Kosmos*. This is what the myth teaches us.

The "vegetarianism" of later Orphism was a shunning of the state sacrifice. Sacrificial animals were always domestic and all slaughter of them was sacrificial. Sacrifice was a societal structure of the Greek city state and to participate in it was to be part of society. Later Orphic mystics lived outside society as itinerants – again a degeneration of the original Orphic current.

While outside society, the Wolf Cult initiates live on hunted meat as "black hunters." They do not perform the societal sacrifice, but perform their own rites to the sound of the howling *aulos* at dusk. Sacrifice serves to remind men of their division from the gods. In the Silver Age, Prometheus first performed this sacrifice, rending gods and men asunder.

The true Orphic current renounces this. The Wolf Cultist seeks to join the gods once again so he may know them. Orpheus shows a way to bridge the gap: the howling void separating men and gods.

This is the way of the warrior band; the wolf pack outside the city, free from the rules of a degenerated society. They are invisible to the rest of society. To be invisible is the way of divinity. The wolf is both invisible and supernatural.

In the Golden Age all men could communicate with gods. Now in this Age of Iron only an initiate, the hero-shaman, can do this. The Wolf Cultist channels the gods in an ecstatic Hyperborean trance.

Later Orphism places the divine spark in Dionysos. Originally Dionysos also represented the entire cycle of rebirth, Apollon the possibility of liberation. Dionysos is *bios*: immortal life; Apollon is transcendence.

Souls are reincarnated in a Cycle of Generation or Wheel of Existence. This cycle of birth, death, and rebirth is revealed to initiates. Dionysos is called Liber, because he liberates the initiate, leading to an Apollonian way of transcendence.

The Neoplatonist Olympiodoros says men perform mystic rites to *"be set free of their lawless ancestry"* (*Orphic Fragment* 232). The Wolf Cultist seeks to cleanse his Spirit of this Titanic element, allowing to remain only the divine spark derived from Dionysos or Bakkhos. To become *Bakkhos* an initiate needs to grasp the significance of these teachings: he has to understand the song.

This is not available to all. Even those who are initiated do not have more than a chance of realisation. This is why in *Orphic Fragment* 235, Olympiodoros states, *"Many are the wand-bearers, but few the Bakkhoi."*

The Hyperborean key to liberation is inside us. To misuse this divine spark within is to secure one's place in the dark Underworld. Initiation is that which gives a true understanding of the *Kosmos* and life. The initiate passes beyond due to his enlightenment, not the ritual of initiation alone.

Initiation into the Mysteries gives an initiate understanding. Like the Tibetan *Book of the Dead*, it provides a map of navigation; but the seeker must still walk this path alone. He must experience the gods in their manifold forms, both benevolent and wrathful, passing beyond by knowing them. He must open the door at each barrier in front of him, ascending to that highest state of Being.

οι Υπερβορείοι Θεοί

The Hyperborean Gods

Modern minds need to distinguish between deities in a way ancients did not. We need to clearly delineate between the personalities of Apollon, Dionysos, Kórē, Dēmḗtēr, etc. These forms are more rigid in the exoteric understanding of the Ancient Greek religion, but the Orphic stream preserves these exoteric deities as avatars of the Hyperborean gods. Once the initiate is familiar with these, he is able to see parallels between ancient gods of the West and those of the East.

The Western tantric tradition recognised a plurality of manifestations and avatars for each god. As the great German scholar Edwin Rhode stated in his seminal work *Psyche*: *"The name and conception of Zeus, Apollo, Hermês, Athena, and all the gods represented innumerable diversities in the myths and rituals of the different cities and races."* Epic reduced these to one Zeus, one Apollon, and so on for the sake of transmission. It left the manifold incarnations of more complex deities to an esoteric current.

While some gods, such as Zeus, subsumed many smaller local deities into his godhead as he encountered them, the canonical set of Greek gods we have been handed down were not all individual deities, but manifestations of higher divine beings: Hyperborean gods.

Dionysos, the deity last to be accepted into the Olympian pantheon, is a hero-god representing a transmutation of chthonic and dark elements to the Olympian light. Dionysos travels to India in his mythos and is linked to Śiva: the male upright, unchangeable element and vehicle for transmutation. Śiva drinks the Kālakūṭa poison to save the world; Dionysos, like Apollon, is a healer who harms.

Dionysos is sacrificed and consumed by the Titans, but is then reborn as a powerful vehicle of immortality for men, as is the Vedic deity Soma, who is killed and consumed in a perpetual cycle. The kentaur nature spirits of Dionysos are the same as Vedic Gandharvas, who are Soma guardians. Both Herakles and Theseus kill kentaurs who get drunk on wine, a Greek telling of the theft of Soma from the Gandharvas.

Dionysos is also a Sacrificial bull who lives again after sacrifice, reenacting the Vedic sacrifice to restore that which has been taken from existence by men. The dismembered Bakkhos is the soul of the world, pluralised in fauna like Vedic Paśupati, Lord of Animals. As Karl Kerényi states in his *Prometheus*: *"The sacrifice offered up by men is a sacrifice of foolhardy thieves, stealers of the divinity round about them."*

The first sacrifice by men is offered by Prometheus, who is Vedic Manu, archetype of man. This sacrifice breaks apart the world of men and gods, creating a broken world of sacrifice that must be reenacted until the *Kosmos* is once more made whole.

Dionysos' manifestation as Zagreus travelled the southern Indo-European route of India – Iran – Anatolia – Krete. The god is a mountain deity, not originally chthonic, but upright like the lingam of Śiva. Dionysos as Sabazios, who is considered a manifestation of Zeus, travelled the northern Indo-European route of Phrygia – Thraki – Northern Greece. These northern and southern Indo-European lineages converged in Greece where the Dionysian manifestations were reunited.

Orphism encodes into its mythology that Phanes, Zeus, and Dionysos are all a continuation of each other. The god is a Light Bearer like Apollon or Iranian Mithra – all intimately connected. Roman Mithras' symbolism is also reflective of this same manifold deity, with key bull-slaying and serpent themes in his mythos and worship. Phanes represents an older incarnation of Apollon-Dionysos before he is split in two by the exoteric tradition.

The Dionysian is a tantric route to the Apollonian. They are two sides of the same coin like Rudra and Śiva. Apollon gathered the remains of Dionysos and took them to his shrine at Delphoi after Dionysos was killed by Titans.

175

Dionysos reigns at Delphoi as Apollon's deputy during his three-month sojourn among the Hyperboreans. It is then that Dionysos' female attendants, his Thyiades ("Awakeners") and Mainades ("Dismemberers"), dance ecstatically over Mount Parnassos.

Apollon and Dionysos also share as attendants the Kouretes (Korybantes/Kabeiroi). These warrior spirits are the Ganas of Śiva. They are the *Tritopatores* of Zeus, souls of ancestors and Wind Spirits like the Vedic *Pitṛs*, *Rudras*, or *Maruts* of Indra.

They are the *Fravaṣis* of Mithra. They are "swarming ghosts" that need to be entertained on the last day of Dionysos' *Anthesteria* festival in spring. These groups are like members of the Germanic *Wild Hunt* of Odin.

This wind connection between Dionysos and Apollon is mediated by Hermês. He is a wind spirit that summons and transports souls of the dead between worlds with his two-forked *rhábdos* wand (not his herald's *kerykeion*). This is a function fulfilled in the Iranian and Vedic tradition by the similarly ambiguous god Vayu.

Dionysos-Śiva is one end of the Pole mediated by Hermês-Vayu. At the other end is Apollon-Rudra: youthful archer, healer who harms, and wind god who shoots from afar. As Apollon Pythios he is a dragon slayer who kills Python, much as Zeus kills the dragon-monster Typhon.

In the Vedic tradition it is Indra who is parallel to Zeus as a dragon slayer, killing the serpent Vṛtra and transforming him into the Dionysian lunar god Soma. The Arrow of Apollon, thunderbolt of Zeus, and *vajra* of Indra are all shafts of light that dispel darkness and vanquish the shadow-monster binding the *Kosmos*.

Walter Otto, in his work *Theophania*, writes: *"The 'Dionysian being' wants intoxication, i.e. closeness; the Apollonian wants clarity and form, i.e. distance, the attitude of the recogniser. Apollon's solar eye rejects the all-too-close, the preoccupation with things, as well as mystical drunkenness and its ecstatic dream. He does not want what we sentimentally call the soul, but the Spirit. This means: freedom, a noble distance, an expanded view. It is the Spirit to which the being of the world speaks, in which all things and beings are reflected as forms."*

Apollon is the god who is far. He is a distant god in the Polar North, only accessible to those who have successfully navigated up the more imminent avatars. As Kallimakhos says in his *Hymn to Apollon*: *"We will see you o worker from afar and we shall never be lowly."*

He is the Hyperborean shamanic god – Spirit of divine inspiration. Apollon's prophets are never fully possessed, but maintain a clarity rather than being in a manic state. They are never totally out of control like their Dionysian counterparts. The shamanic nature of his prophets is reflected in the head of Orpheus, which continues to prophesy mantic utterings.

In the Germanic Odinic tradition the head of a prophet still speaks after being disembodied. Odin carries the head of Mímir with him for divinatory purpose. Apollon goes beyond this though, and as Karl Kerenyi put it in his *Pythagoras and Orpheus*: *"In Apollo's figure, Germanic mythology's Odin of Bitter Death is in union with the White Swan Knight of Sweet Death – Lohengrin."*

The Northern nature of Apollon is also evident through his connection with the Hyperborean number seven. The number seven is associated with the Northern Bear constellation. This stellar arrangement never dips below the Northern horizon.

The bear is female, hence the connection of the bear with Apollon's sister Artemis. The Greeks counted seven stars in the Pleiades constellation, and these were companion nymphs of Artemis. Both Apollon and Artemis have seven letters in their names, while Apollon has seven strings on his lyre.

Apollon was born on the seventh day of *Thargelion*. He visits Delos on the seventh day of *Anthesterion*. The *Karneia* festival of Apollon is on the seventh day of the month of *Karneios*. His *Hyakinthia* festival is on the seventh day of *Hekatombeion*. The Pythian summer festival is on the seventh day of *Bukation*.

Offerings are made to Apollon on the seventh day of every month. He is called Apollon *Hebdomagetes* ("Commander of Sevens"). Seven Wise men from Greece wrote the Delphic Maxims at his holy sanctuary.

In Northern shamanism there are seven celestial levels to ascend through. There are likewise seven planetary spheres. Seven is explicitly connected to shamanic practice in the Altai region. It is a Hyperborean number with the seventh heaven of Apollon at its summit.

The Hyperborean shaman Orpheus teaches there were seven male and seven female Titans, rather than the usual six. These seven Titans rend Dionysos into seven pieces. Thus seven is connected with the Underworld aspect of the Hyperborean god Apollon: with Dionysos.

Descent into the Underworld is a Hyperborean shamanic act, as is ascent up the Cosmic Mountain, under Ursa Major, to greet the Wolf Light. Orpheus' life ends with his ascent up the mountain to worship Apollon. Before this, he had already descended into the Underworld to retrieve the goddess.

In counterbalance to an upright, unmoving male is a female who brings all into manifestation through union with the masculine. This creative energy in the Vedic tradition is Śakti; she is counterpart to Śiva.

All goddesses are manifestations of Śakti, the cosmic energy running through all existence. The Greek manifestations of the goddess are similarly connected, even at times interchangeable. They are avatars of the great Mountain Goddess, the divine feminine who is in union with the cosmic mountain, lingam, Pole, and uprightness.

The goddess can appear in the form of the mother: Rhea, or Dēmétēr. The Orphic *Fragmenta* tells us that Rhea becomes Dēmétēr in the Zeus *Kosmos*. Zeus is born from Rhea (who has "many names"), but after swallowing and regurgitating the *Kosmos* he sires Persephónē with Dēmétēr – who was Rhea.

Rhea is in turn also an aspect of Gaîa the Earth Mother. This all-giving and nurturing mother is also called Pandóra, giver of "all gifts" as her name tells us. Gaîa is also Themis, a goddess who was enthroned at Delphoi before Apollon.

Semelē, the second mother of Dionysos (the "son of earth and sky") is also an Earth Mother. *Métēr* ("mother") can also be *Maîa* ("grandmother"). This is the name of the mother of Hermês, who is son of Zeus. The upright male principle manifests himself through a motherly female principle.

The mother also manifests herself though this interaction and creates *Kórē* ("maiden"). Thus Dēmétēr creates another avatar of herself in Persephónē. Kórē is fated in her kindly form to become *Nýmphē* ("bride"). She is destined to go through the cycles of femininity from maiden to grandmother in an eternal cycle of manifestation.

Both nurturing mother and welcoming maiden have opposite aspects. Ancient to the gods, Hekátē is a dark mother like the Indian goddess Kālī; Artemis is the dark maiden who kills any who try to violate her maidenhood. While different in many ways, she is also kindred to Durgā, the martial and fierce goddess. Durgā-Kālī are the same goddess in Indic lore while in Orphism, Hekátē-Artemis are the same. This dual manifestation of a goddess is outside the cycle of regeneration.

Hekátē is a mediator deity as queen of souls who are eastbound to the upper world. Underworld Hermês is her masculine counterpart. Both are featured at Samothráki, as well as having a role in Eleusís.

Hekátē appears at night in moonlight at crossroads – both Hermês attributes. She is accompanied by her "crew" of female souls who have not been given proper burial or were killed violently. They are carried on the wind, which is also associated with Hermês/Vayu.

Hekátē has several avatars of her own. These include Gorgyra (Gorgo), Mormo, Lamia, Gella, and Empousa the ghost of midday. All are female underworld deities.

The Gorgon is a fearsome side of the Great Mother, thus Hekátē-Gorgo is this very avatar: a bogey to scare away evil. The Hero must pass Gorgons and Graiai to reach Hyperborea, thus passing the test of this fearsome incarnation of the goddess.

The souls who make up the company of Hekátē along with her *daímonaic* pack of hounds are the furious host. This is connected to the Greek Wild Hunt led by Artemis as huntress. Artemis and Hekátē are one and the same in Orphic tradition.

Artemis is likewise a maiden, but a violent and inviolable one. The goddess Athena is the foster mother of heroes, but also a virgin. She is the Kórē of warriors, born from Zeus' head. She is the manifestation of Reason and Light.

The aspects of god and goddess fade into dual Beings to an initiate. He is able to understand what he encounters through a binary lens of Zeus' *Kosmos*. This appears as the Underworld to he who is ritually dead.

As a free Spirit in a world of ghosts, he recognises the signs others do not. He sees forms of the gods in everything and is able to navigate the pillars of light, ladders, and wheels by embodying guardian deities who appear before him.

The labyrinth symbolizes the mother goddess and earthly rebirth: it is the Underworld. Those who do not have a flash of light to illuminate passageways through this maze are doomed to wander manifestation for eternity. The elite initiation into Hyperborean Mysteries gives the seeker a beacon to follow so he can exit the labyrinth and ascend the Cosmic Mountain.

He goes beyond Zeus, Dionysos, Hermês, and Apollon; beyond Nyx, Rhea, Dēmétēr, Persephónē, Kórē, Artemis, Hekátē, and Athena. Beyond the gods lies the original primal unity of the *Kosmos* of Phanes. Beyond the gods, as *metátheos*, as *atideva*, an initiate may utter the Orphic exclamation: *"I have flown out of the weary wheel."*

η Ψυχή καί ο Δαίμων

Soul and Spirit

Man has both soul and Spirit, but these can be difficult to separate in the Greek sources. As in earlier works, both were referred to as *psykhḗ*; however, in the later Socratic tradition, another word was used to refer to the Spirit: *daímōn*. This originally meant "god" in an impersonal sense – as opposed to *theós*, which was used to refer to a specific god. Through the development of philosophical language, a term was used that better suited the concept of Spirit.

Although man has both, the soul dissolves with a body, entering the Underworld as an *eídōlon* ("image") of the personal dead. The Spirit is a *spark* of divinity that is "reincarnated" until it is "liberated." The Buddhist tradition has an apt metaphor in the form of a string of *mālā* beads used to count *mantra* recitation. The individual life is a bead on the *mālā*, while Spirit is the string holding them together. To take an *ātmanic* rather than *anātmanic* approach: the thread of divine Spirit strings together a series of souls in a Cycle of Generation.

This is expressed in the Samothrakian Twins. An earthly twin is a current human soul entering the Mysteries to find its celestial twin: its Spirit. This celestial twin is associated with the serpent, the string of the *mālā*. Thus the Orphic phrase: *"I am a child of Earth and starry Heaven; But my race is of Heaven (alone)."*

Through the *pneuma* (a latent physical form of primordial spirit essence – the "life force") a soul is connected with Dionysos. This is the very real *bíos* ("life") residing in a human being. It is both divine and of earth, having an Underworldly character. It is of this material plane, but also a mediator; a "liberator" like Dionysos.

The soul is a medium through which we may commune with a higher Spirit that is celestial and Apollonian. It is a mountain that must be scaled in order to greet a dawning realisation cresting its summit like the sun, illuminating the seeker. This is an immanentisation of one's *daímōn*.

The soul must be sublimated to Spirit in an alchemical transformation allowing an initiate to complete his Great Work of Dionysian Apollonism. Through it he is able to reclaim his original divine seat beyond the gods in Hyperborea.

η επιστροφή στην υπερβορεία

Return to Hyperborea

The man who does not free himself from the Cycle of Generation is fated to be put through endless rounds of reincarnation. He who makes himself *Bakkhos* can become an immortal who goes beyond the gods, past the Hyperborean state of Phanes. He journeys to the original state of Being outside the *Kosmoi* of both Zeus and Phanes, free to travel through time and space unfettered by gods, Temporality, or Necessity.

We are from beyond the Light World of Phanes, reborn of Dionysian-Titanic remnants. We must trace of our way back to our origin by purging the Titanic, and with the guidance of Hermês following the Dionysian via an Underworldly realm of Kórē to the Apollonian Celestial. We cannot be reabsorbed into Zeus; we must travel beyond the gods to the Light World of Phanes, reassuming our original form as men of the Golden Age. Only in this capacity can we hope to achieve *atideva-metátheos*.

Mythos is cultus, cultus is mythos. They are inseparable and the same. We live myth through our daily acts, words, and revelations. The Underworld is now, and the punishments are states of being caused by lesser impulses.

We must rise from this tomb of material existence, exiting the Underworld by charming Kórē. By becoming *Bakkhos* we begin an Olympian journey of ascent, a Return to Hyperborea. However we must also return Hyperborea to the world, reinstating a Golden Age within hearts of men.

The Wolf Initiate is not driven by others; rather he is fuelled by his inner fire. He is wary of the horizontal, rejecting a slavery of the oblique. He recalls his ancestors, honours the gods, and reaches upward. Waging an inner war, he fights to bring his being into total alignment – striving for complete liberation at all times, ready for what is beyond both life and death.

Following a golden sunlight illuminating mysterious amber roads to the North on a path of return, an initiate seeks the master key unlocking the chakras of an invisible earth. He ascends a Hyperborean Mountain in the Wolf Light to greet the dawn and witness an illuminating light of realisation. He treads a tantric Path of the Gods to a region of thunderbolts beyond the door of the sun. We are not Hyperboreans; we are men of this earth and time, and therefore cannot act as immortals. In this Dark Age, this Kali Yuga, only the Tantra of Orpheus is appropriate.

The universe manifests in man, who is a microcosm of a macrocosm. Higher in nature than gods, being both mortal and divine, existing and non-existing, only man can reach for supertheistic liberation. Through virile action, an iron will for heroic struggle, and steadfast determination, man is able to steer his own path through hazards and pitfalls of this world, attaining the Summit.

The Wolf Initiate is a priest-warrior. He is a lord of spear and sacrifice. He is a tender of fire, mediator of his relationship with the supernatural: the principal which brings gods to life.

The initiate holds his destiny in his hands, deity standing in the form of man. To navigate his way on the Hyperborean path, to exercise his divine right from above, he must occupy the immutability of the middle. There is no beginning or end – the Cycle Of Generation is endless.

The direction of initiation is vertical. This is the only escape from the rotation of the wheel. The Heroic Initiate must make his way to the axis, becoming a Lord of the Centre around which all turns – imposing his righteous, aristocratic will.

Having drunk from the Spring of Memory, an initiate stands upright, erect, receiving and transmitting revelation on the vertical plane. He becomes an axis where Higher Order is manifested. Motionless, the pivot point remains steadfast as the masses under the weight of the wheel perpetually chase their tails, unaware of their ability to transcend.

In the centre, time stands still. The midnight sun rotates around a motionless axis while the Heroic Initiate of an Ancient and Noble Wolf Cult works his magic. Crowned with celestial fire he sits at a crossroad of worlds. Occupying this middle realm, with one eye looking to the underworld he reaches upward embodying the Vertical, the Pole, the World Tree.

Enter the Mysteries. Drink from the Spring of Memory. Know Thyself. Master the Wolf. Return to Hyperborea.

RETURN TO HYPERBOREA

Was written by Tom Billinge.

Learn more about Tom at **TomBillinge.com**.

If you enjoyed this book, consider reading *WarYoga*, also by Tom Billinge, and *The Aryan Männerbund: Studies on Indo-Iranian Language and Religious History* by Stig Wikander.

Watch for future releases by Tom and other authors from Sanctus Arya Press.

EX UMBRA IN SOLEM

Tom at the Sanctuary of the Great Gods in Samothrace, Greece

About the Author

Tom Billinge is originally from England and lives in the USA. He grew up surrounded by Ancient Greek mythology, culture, archaeology and history, as his father was a historical geographer and his mother was Greek. After graduating with a degree in archaeology, Tom moved to Asia, where he explored temples and immersed himself in the martial and spiritual traditions of the East.

Following several years travelling the world and writing for a living, Tom returned to the West and to his roots. This led to his first book, *Undying Glory: The Solar Path of Greek Heroes* that examines the first heroes of Greek mythology. Tom then continued the series with an exploration of the Homeric material in *Age of Heroes: Beyond the Solar Path*. The final book of the trilogy, *Return to Hyperborea: The Heroic Initiate*, examines the Orphic tradition.

With a particular interest in Indo-European matters, Tom spends much of his time making connections between the spiritual and martial impulses of the various Indo-European cultures. His book *WarYoga* explores the Indic branch of the Indo-European physical alchemical practice, while the sequel, *WarYoga: Zurxāne* deals with the Iranian tradition. The forthcoming third part, *WarYoga: Palaistra* will be released in 2025. These works are the culmination of years of academic, spiritual, and physical research.

Tom has also translated several works including the Iranian epic *Garšaspname*, and *The Aryan Männerbund* by Stig Wikander. *Varuna-Ouranos* and *The Feast of Immortality* by Georges Dumezil, *Pythagoras and Orpheus* by Karl Kerenyi, *Theophania* by Walter Otto are slated for future release by Sanctus Arya Press.

In addition to authoring books, articles, and essays, he teaches Muay Thai, Jiu Jitsu, Old English bareknuckle, Ancient Greek Pankration, and works as an editor in combat sports media. Tom is a Fellow of the Royal Asiatic Society.

For more information about Tom Billinge and his work, visit his website at **TomBillinge.com**.